Raising An Anxious Child: A Parental Guide to Raising Anxiety Free Children in the 21st Century

ABOUT THE AUTHOR

As a parent myself, I know how hard it is to take care of your family. Raising your kids in a nearly perfect environment is the dream of every parent. Yet, it is a hard nut to crack, and things become even more difficult when one or more of our children suffer from anxieties. Sometimes, the anxiety is just a passing moment, but it can become extremely tough to keep things smooth as a parent when a kid has clinical anxiety. Take it from a parent who has all the experiences in raising an anxious child. My paternal drive helped me gather the most authentic resources that helped my child overcome the issues with his anxiety personality. Those strategies have proven highly beneficial in removing the fears from my child's life gradually. It is my responsibility to share my experiences with parents like you. That is why I wrote this book. Everything included in this book was a game-changer for me, and I can confidently say that it will be a game-changer for you too.

© Copyright 2021 Rosa Newman - All rights reserved.

The content contained within this book may not be reproduced, duplicated or transmitted without direct written permission from the author or the publisher.

Under no circumstances will any blame or legal responsibility be held against the publisher, or author, for any damages, reparation, or monetary loss due to the information contained within this book. Either directly or indirectly. You are responsible for your own choices, actions, and results.

Legal Notice:

This book is copyright protected. This book is only for personal use. You cannot amend, distribute, sell, use, quote or paraphrase any part, or the content within this book, without the consent of the author or publisher.

Disclaimer Notice:

Please note the information contained within this document is for educational and entertainment purposes only. All effort has been executed to present accurate, up to date, and reliable, complete information. No warranties of any kind are declared or implied. Readers acknowledge that the author is not engaging in the rendering of legal, financial, medical or professional advice. The content within this book has been derived from various sources. Please consult a licensed professional before attempting any techniques outlined in this book.

By reading this document, the reader agrees that under no circumstances is the author responsible for any losses, direct or indirect, which are incurred as a result of the use of the information contained within this document, including, but not limited to, — errors, omissions, or inaccuracies.

SPECIAL BONUS!

Want this bonus book for free?

Get FREE unlimited access to it and all of my new books by joining the Fan Base!

  SCAN W/YOUR CAMERA TO JOIN!

Table of contents

INTRODUCTION 1

CHAPTER 1: ANXIETY MADE SIMPLE 3

Anxiety as a problem 4

Basic symptoms of anxiety 5

Our bodies and adrenaline 6

1. Shallow and fast breath 7
2. Dizzy head 7
3. Hijacked brain 8
4. Body sweats 8
5. Racing heartbeat 8
6. Jelly arms and legs 9
7. Need to pee … again 9

Are anxiety and depression frequent among children, and do they go away? 10

What is the prevalence of anxiety and depression among children? 10

Will they be able to overcome it? 11

Is it true that anxiety and depression are dangerous to my child? ... 11

What is my child's prognosis? 13

CHAPTER 2: WHAT FACTORS INFLUENCE THE DEVELOPMENT OF DEPRESSION AND ANXIETY IN CHILDREN AND TEENAGERS? 15

Personality and genetics 15

Learning factor 17

Listening to people saying worrying and concerned things 18

Life experiences 19

Who is to blame for my child's behavior? 21

Case of stage fright 22

CHAPTER 3: THE EIGHT TYPES OF ANXIETIES 26

Specific (simple) phobia 27

Social phobia 28

Separation anxiety 29

Generalized anxiety disorder 29

Panic disorder 30

Agoraphobia 30

Hallway panic (mdm) 31

Obsessive-compulsive disorder (ocd) 31

Post-traumatic stress disorder (ptsd) 32

CHAPTER 4: LEARNING TO THINK REALISTICALLY 34

The fundamentals of realistic thinking 34

The interaction between events, thoughts, and feelings 35

Two common thinking mistakes 36

1. Overestimating probability 36

2. Overestimating consequences 37

Activity for parents- finding proof of my own concern................... 38

Teaching your child about realistic thinking 42

Why are thoughts important?.. 43

The detective approach 44

How to teach your child detective thinking 46

A final point to consider 51

Why are thoughts important?.. 52

Harry's story 53

Mike's story 53

Self-talk 54

Use detective thinking for bigger issues 55

CHAPTER 5: DIFFERENT PROFESSIONALS, ONE GOAL 58

Psychologists 58

Clinical psychologist 58

Counseling psychologist 59

Educational psychologist 59

Psychiatrists 60

Counselors and therapists 60

Camhs workers and primary mental health workers 61

Psychiatric nurses 61

CHAPTER 6: WHAT KIND OF THERAPY WILL BE GIVEN TO MY CHILD? 62

Cognitive behaviour therapy 62

What is cognitive behaviour therapy? 63

Interpersonal therapy 65

Family therapy 65

Counseling 66

Psychodynamic therapies 66

Support groups and self-help 67

CHAPTER 7: STRATEGIES FOR PARENTS 68

Dealing with anxiety in children in unhelpful ways 69

Reassuring your child too much 69

Being too involved and directive 71

Permitting avoidance 71

Becoming impatient with your child 71

Rewarding brave, non-anxious behavior 72

Teaching your child about rewards 75

Ignoring behaviors that you don't want 76

Prompting your child to cope constructively 76

Modeling brave, non-anxious behavior 77

CHAPTER 8: ESSENTIAL THINGS TO KEEP IN MIND WHEN DEALING WITH ANXIOUS CHILDREN 79

Being consistent 79

Keeping your emotions in check 79

Distinguishing between anxious and naughty behavior 80

A few fundamentals that can make a big difference 81

Diet 81

Low blood sugar 82

Caffeine 83

Sleep 83

Routines 85

Exercise 86

CHAPTER 9: THE SEVEN CONFIDENT THOUGHTS 88

Step one – special time 89

Special time: 10 minutes quiz 90

Step 2 – have a good time with your family. 92

Communicating nasty surprises 93

Good co-parenting 95

Discuss, discuss, discuss 96

Compromise, compromise, compromise 96

CHAPTER 10: BOOSTING YOUR CHILD'S SELF-ESTEEM AND CONFIDENCE 100

Make the most of your child's abilities. 101

So, what do i have to do? 102

Push them to try new things 102

CHAPTER 11: BEHAVIORAL MODIFICATIONS TO MANAGE AN ANXIOUS CHILD 104

Learning to control poor and nervous behavior 104

Ignoring 106

The rules for ignoring 107

When should i use ignorance? 107

When should i not use ignorance? 107

So, where do i go from here? 108

Managing potentially harmful and damaging behaviors: 110

Time out 110

Dealing with non-compliance: what happens if you don't follow the rules? 112

Consequences 113

Consequences and how to manage them 113

Beneficial consequences 114

Negative consequences 115

CHAPTER 12: DEALING WITH WORRY AND FEARS 118

Fears 119

Avoidance 119

Treating miranda 121

The fight-flight response 123

Tips for dealing with fears 125

Worries 128

Dealing with realistic worries 129

Dealing with unrealistic worries 129

CONCLUSION 132

REFERENCES 134

INTRODUCTION

In this modern age of ever-increasing worry, it's getting more difficult for parents to know what constitutes a healthy level of anxiety in their children and an alarming situation. Kids confront various obstacles at various phases of development, ranging from nightmares in toddlers to separation anxiety and tummy troubles in primary school children. Moreover, self-conscious adolescents find social situations unsettling and can lead to recurrent episodes of clinical anxiety.

Anxieties are common in children, and the issue can persist even after reaching puberty. Everyone suffers from anxiety, which results from our "tricky" survival brains attempting to cope with life's ever-changing demands. A primary method for understanding anxiety is, to sum up, all the things that lead to worries and cause stress in children. When you understand the causes and types of anxiety in your children, you can then remove your child's views and beliefs regarding their ability to deal with the anxieties. Most parents mismanage the anxiety issues in their children, and as a result, their child's anxiety levels can be increased. In simple words, a child's anxiety management strategies determine whether they thrive in their daily lives or have significant difficulties welcoming new experiences.

Your reaction to your child's anxiousness will significantly impact how they cope with the issue. Thanks to your support and guidance, parents like you have the key to anchoring their children with safety and a healthy connection. You and your child may build on this solid foundation by working together on problem-solving skills to help them cope with their anxieties.

That's why you must be able to recognize when your child's anxiety is affecting their everyday life and learning abilities.

CHAPTER 1: ANXIETY MADE SIMPLE

Question: What is anxiety, and is it a normal condition?

Answer: Everyone experiences anxiety from time to time. It's natural to feel nervous when meeting some new people, riding a rollercoaster, being asked to speak in class, or waiting for an interview. Some children only feel anxious when something is really out of their comfort zone, while others often feel it. It is also relevant to the personality type possessed by a child.

When anxiety strikes, you'll be aware that something isn't quite right, but you may not be able to articulate what's going on. This is true in the case of children and teens. You may be concerned that something horrible may happen to you or someone you love. You could be angry or unhappy and want to avoid doing things, or you might just want to stay at home.

Anxiety is the body's natural alert mechanism, which has historically aided human survival. It works so effectively that it activates even when we don't need it, such as when we assume there is a danger when there isn't any, or when we begin to wonder, "What if something dreadful happens?"

People who are nervous monitor for danger and hyper-aware of their bodies as alarm signals are more prone to recurrent anxiety attacks.

This is why anxiety can be so draining for them!

Anxiety is not an indication that anything is wrong or that you are weak. It's an indication that your healthy, robust brain is doing precisely what it's supposed to do to keep you safe. Anxiety is unconcerned with whether the threat is genuine or imagined because our brain prefers to keep us secure.

Sometimes our brain goes to extended limits in trying to protect us. When this happens, it sets off a chain reaction of weird feelings in our bodies. When we feel bad, we get anxious thoughts, making us even more nervous. It is like a vicious cycle. It's as if we're ready for action, but there's no enemy, so the tension builds up in our bodies without having a chance to be let out!

Anxiety as a problem

Anxiety becomes problematic when it affects a child's sense of who they are, relationships, and engagement with school and other activities. Anxiety becomes a problem when a child's worries, whether their thoughts, feelings or physical sensations, make them avoid situations, limiting their learning and restricting the joyful experience of life.

Distinguishing anxiety from usual fears is essential. Throughout childhood, we all naturally experience transient concerns that arise in line with our ability to recognize and understand potential dangers in our environment.

When a child is young, fears seem to be immediate and tangible, like separation from a loved one or a fear of strangers. As the child gets older, worries become more abstract, centering on thoughts that anticipate problems ('what if?') and focusing on the less tangible (bad dreams, someone getting hurt, or struggling at school). Children are expected to grow out of many of these fears as they develop.

Sadly, this is more difficult for some children than for others, which is why it's essential to focus on what is happening in your child's world. Suppose you feel that anxiety is having a significant impact on your child's daily life and ability to function. In that case, it may be time to seek some professional support in guiding you and your child forward.

Basic symptoms of anxiety

Many children experience the issues mentioned below at some point, but if your child has been experiencing one or more of these symptoms regularly for the previous six months, it's time to see your doctor.

Your local doctor can provide you with information about trusted local support programs. A psychologist, psychotherapist, play therapist, or counselor are examples of these professionals who can assist you and your child. Recurrent anxiety and worry about several events or activities can be triggered because of the following issues:

- Difficulty falling or staying asleep.
- restlessness.
- insufficient sleep.
- Irritability.
- Muscle tension.
- Depression.
- Difficulties at school, in social settings, or interacting with people.

Other potential reasons for anxiety, such as physical illnesses, pharmaceutical side effects, drug or alcohol usage, and any other mental health difficulties, will be ruled out by your doctor.

Our bodies and adrenaline

When you're worried, your body reacts in a variety of ways for a myriad of purposes. There's nothing to fight or hide from when there's nothing to fight over. Flight-Freeze adrenaline is the gasoline that's coursing through your veins.

Adrenaline is a stress hormone responsible for getting you up and moving for various reasons, including excitement, reaching a deadline, or competing in a race. This massive burst of energy enables us to perform at our best. When we're concerned, scared, or threatened, adrenaline rushes into our bodies since there's no deadline to meet or race to run, and there's nowhere for it to go.

Here are some of the things you could experience when your adrenaline levels rise, as well as the reasons behind this hormonal rush.

1. Shallow and fast breath

What's going on? Your brain tells your body to quit wasting oxygen by sending it to your muscles so they can fight or run instead of using it on forceful and deep breaths.

This is how you could be feeling—your breathing shifts from long, leisurely breaths to quick, shallow breaths. You may feel puffy or out of breath. It's possible that your cheeks will flush red, and your face will feel heated.

2. Dizzy head

What exactly is going on here? If you don't fight or flee, your body's oxygen levels rise, and your carbon dioxide levels fall due to your rapid breathing.

If you're dizzy, disoriented, or unwell, you should quickly reassess the situation. Children often show this symptom when they have anxiety attacks.

3. Hijacked brain

What's happening here? Other emotions, such as anger or sadness, may become amplified due to an anxious adrenaline surge.
 It's challenging to think appropriately using the prefrontal cortex, your brain's rational, soothing area, while your thoughts are rushing.

This is how you could be feeling. You may feel enraged or melancholy as if you want to cry for no apparent reason. The prefrontal cortex, your brain's "smart leader," shuts down.

4. Body sweats

What's happening? Your body cools by sweating itself down as if you have to fight or run away. How might you feel? Clammy or sweaty, even if it's cold out.

5. Racing heartbeat

What's happening? Your pulse rises, and your hearts start to beat faster to get the oxygen around your body, especially to the arms and legs, allowing you to run away or attack. Your heart can feel like it's racing, and you might also feel sick. This can feel scary, like a heart attack.

It's OK, though – you're perfectly safe.

6. Jelly arms and legs

Fuel is shunted to your bigger muscles in the arms (in case you need to fight) and the legs (if you need to run away). Your arms and legs might feel tight or wobbly.

7. Need to pee ... again

Adrenaline might make you want to go to the bathroom. We know it happens, but we have no idea why.

As though you have a full bladder and need to empty it. The digestive system locks down so that the energy necessary to digest meals may be utilized by your arms and legs if you need to fight or flee.

It's as though you've got butterflies in your stomach. You may also feel nauseous as if you're about to vomit, and your mouth may feel dry.

With all of this going on in your body, it's no surprise that as the adrenaline wears off, you'll feel weary, shaky, and weak!

Are anxiety and depression frequent among children, and do they go away?

What is the prevalence of anxiety and depression among children?

What is the prevalence of anxiety disorders? Anxiety and sadness are pretty widespread during childhood and much more so during puberty. Indeed, anxiety is now broadly accepted as the most frequent psychiatric disease in childhood, with depression following closely after.

Estimates of how frequent anxiety and depression occurs vary significantly based on the children investigated, the nation in which they live, and the method used to quantify fear and sadness. However, in recent and excellent research of children in the United Kingdom, about 4% of children were found to have an anxiety condition, and nearly 1% were clinically depressed.

Although this may not appear to be a large number, it indicates that one or two children in a class of thirty will be anxious or depressed.

These illnesses have been reported to be considerably more prevalent in other investigations.

Furthermore, these investigations provide a single snapshot in time. In studies that have measured 11 children every few years until they are grown up, many children have shown up as being depressed or anxious at some point in their life.

Will they be able to overcome it?

Some children go through an extremely nervous or sad period and then, thankfully, grow out of it.

This is especially true if they are only suffering from a minor episode of anxiety or depression. However, this relief can be temporary. They can suffer from anxiety and depression for the rest of their lives unless they are treated. Recent research also points to the fact that most people who have clinical anxieties had a depressive or anxious childhood. It is essential to consider an anxious or sad child seriously for this reason alone.

Is it true that anxiety and depression are dangerous to my child?

Are anxiety and depression the same thing? Some children will be able to overcome an emotional disorder or condition with no long-term repercussions. Untreated anxiety or depression as a youngster, on the other hand, might leave scars for the unfortunate.

We know that such children frequently fail to achieve their academic potential; it is difficult to focus when you are depressed, or your head is flooded with worrying thoughts.

Similarly, childhood should be a period of learning how to make friends and get along with others.

Some children who are too worried or sad may suffer from loneliness, and they can miss out on friendships and social skills that are useful in later years. People who approach adulthood without these skills are at risk of being lonely, leading to increased anxiety and despair.

Similarly, we believe that some nervous or depressed teens might learn to use alcohol or, in rare cases, illicit narcotics to help calm their emotions. This can lead to issues with alcohol or drugs in some circumstances (but certainly not all). Last but not least, a word of warning.

Highly anxious and very nervous children might become so desperate that they injure themselves and even attempt suicide in rare circumstances. If you have any cause to believe your child is considering self-harm, you should see your doctor right away. If your child ever suggests that they could damage themselves in the near future (i.e., before you can get to the doctor), you should take them to the local Accident & Emergency Hospital right away. Remember to have the emergency and accident services on speed dial.

What is my child's prognosis?

Although anxious and depressive children might have various issues, their chances of recovery are high if they receive appropriate therapy early on.

Many adolescents and teenagers who appear to be emotionally impaired may go on to enjoy happily and fulfilled lives.

Anita was referred to CAMHS when she was 15 years old (Child and Adolescent Mental Health Services). She'd been refusing to attend school for about four months and was on the verge of being housebound. Sally, Anita's mother, was worried about her and tried all she could to get her out of the home and school. Sally was growing irritated with Anita since none of her persuading's had succeeded. Sally's school was threatening to expel her.

Luckily, they found help from a therapist who told Sally that her daughter has clinical anxiety. On further investigations, the therapist found that Anita was doing self-harm. Timely management successfully cured the anxiety issues in Anita. She is now living a happy and healthy life.

In conclusion, while many children experience periods of anxiety and even misery, most of them go on to achieve great success. Those who do not fully heal, on the other hand, may face a great deal of suffering.

Furthermore, they may face difficulties in adulthood. As a result, you should seek professional aid for your child as soon as possible.

CHAPTER 2: WHAT FACTORS INFLUENCE THE DEVELOPMENT OF DEPRESSION AND ANXIETY IN CHILDREN AND TEENAGERS?

'Nobody actually knows' is the most honest response to this question. However, we do have some decent ideas about what contributes to our anxiety or depression. In the vast majority of children, a variety of factors contribute to their anxiety or depression. I'll go through some of the elements that have been investigated in the context of anxiety and depression. If you have ever heard about anxiety and depression in an adult, you will encounter the same themes. This is because we do not believe there is much difference between disorders in children and adults.

Personality and genetics

We know that our genes influence our likelihood of being anxious or depressed. Some individuals are simply born confident and outgoing, and they appear to be able to cope with life's ups and downs, even if they have had rough lives that would appear to be bound to cause these issues. On the other side, some people seem to have perfect lives, with everything going their way - a loving family, academic achievement, a large social circle, and plenty of money – yet they nonetheless suffer from anxiety or depression. The truth is that these folks were most likely created differently from the start.

We also know that infants are born with a portion of their personalities already formed. It is primarily due to their DNA. We believe that certain people are more prone to feeling nervous or sad than others. An example of this may be seen in the case study below.

Sarah and Jason have two children together. Katie, their first child, was laid-back and upbeat from the minute she was born. She didn't weep a lot and was readily consoled. She seemed to like being among a large group of people and was adaptable to changes in her schedule.

When Joe arrived, though, things changed drastically.

Sarah and Jason handled Joe the same way they had treated Katie, but he was a very different person. He wept a lot and was difficult to console. He disliked being in the company of others and struggled when his parents held him. When his routine was disrupted, he struggled to adjust.

They tried visiting a therapist who concluded that both these children had different personality types. Joe was more reserved, and it was hard for him to cope with the changes. The therapist warned Sarah and Jason that their son could develop clinical anxiety if he didn't get any treatment at the earliest. With a bit of understanding and some changes in handling, Joe started doing really well with his life.

I've lost track of how often parents have told me the following incident about two children in the same family who were entirely different from the day they were born. People assumed that children were born with "blank slates" and their upbringing would shape their entire personality. This is just not true, as we now know. From the moment they are born, children have distinct personalities. We know that confident children are born with sensitive characters, making them more vulnerable to anxiety and depression. Joe was one of these children, and he finally sought treatment at the clinic due to his extreme concern.

Learning factor

What is the best way for children to learn to be adults? It's actually not that difficult. They achieve so by observing and imitating the actions of the adults in their environment. How often have you noticed your youngster imitating your actions or hearing them say something using your exact words?

One of the moms who attended our meeting for parents of nervous children told me this humorous incident.

Emily admitted to being a bit of a perfectionist. She took great delight in keeping her home pristine and well-presented. In an atypical moment of gossip, she once told one of her friends that she had been in another friend's toilet (let's name this person Shane) and that it was filthy.

Emily's daughter, Claudia, was calmly playing in the corner, seemingly unconcerned. She was, nevertheless, paying attention. Claudia triumphantly returned from a trip to Shane's house several days later, exclaiming for all to hear, "you're right, Mummy, that toilet is filthy"...!

When I asked Emily what she had taken away from the episode, she stated that it had taught her that children often imitate their parents. She was now mindful that she was soaking in everything even when Claudia didn't appear to be paying attention.

Two forms of learning might teach anxious or depressed behavior to children:

Listening to people saying worrying and concerned things

We conduct a ludicrous exercise where one of us pretends to be a frantic parent who is afraid to go to the dentist when we lead sessions for parents of small children. There is a lot of overacting going on, and none of us will ever win an Oscar. There is a lot of crying and weeping about how awful the dentist will be. How much it will hurt, and "Oh my gosh, the drill!" and other such things. It all comes to a head when we call to cancel the dental appointment. It mostly amuses the parents in the group, but there is a significant point to be made.

After we've finished acting, we ask the parents to describe what a child might learn from seeing their parents work in this manner.

They usually say that the child learned that:

- Dentists are nasty.
- You should avoid going to the dentist.
- Going to the dentist hurts.
- Your mother can't cope.
- If you're scared, the best way to deal with it is to get upset, wail and scream, and think about the worst possible thing that could happen.
- If you're afraid of something, the best thing to do is to stay away from it.

All of the evidence indicates that the parents in our group are correct.

When children hear their parents worried about something frightening, they develop a fear of it as well.

Life experiences

In addition to genes and learning, certain childhood events can make particular children more prone to anxiety and depression. These are mostly life lessons that educate a youngster that the world is a dangerous place.

A major accident, being the victim of a violent attack, or seeing domestic violence can all jeopardize a child's perception of the world as a safe place.

Instead, they believe that the world is hazardous and should begin to be on the lookout for danger. When someone is always on high alert for trouble, they will feel worried, eventually leading to depression.

If your child has been exposed to or observed any traumatic incidents, it can take a toll on your child's health. These situations might be contributing to their anxiety or depression. If this has occurred, I highly suggest you consult your doctor, as your child may require specific counseling to help them cope with what has happened. You can do a lot as a parent to help your child's environment feel secure again. This will be discussed later in the book.

It doesn't necessarily take a significant traumatic occurrence for a youngster to view the world as unsafe and dangerous. I've observed some sensitive children who can feel unsafe as a result of ordinary tensions. If you have a sensitive temperament, you will respond worse than other children if you are often scolded, spanked, or if your environment is unpredictably chaotic.

To put it another way, if you just live in an average, busy, stressed-out household as we all do, you may get nervous or sad.

On the other hand, parents may do a lot to support a child in this situation so that the sensitive child can cope better with the environment.

Who is to blame for my child's behavior?

Usually, no one is to blame. Parents should almost never be held responsible for their children's emotional issues. Even though you recognize yourself at fault in some of the situations, you are not to blame for your child's behavior. There isn't such a thing as an ideal parent. Furthermore, as Sarah and Jason learned, the same parenting might result in one child succeeding and the other struggling. Do not be embarrassed if your youngster has difficulties. When their child is suffering, many parents express embarrassment at seeing other people's children doing well.

They don't realize that all children are born differently, and if other people had tried to raise their children, they would have found it just as hard.

As a result, most psychologists don't hold parents responsible for their children's anxiety or depression. Even though parents do not generally create these issues, we feel that they may do a lot to assist their children in overcoming them.

Case of stage fright

One of my friends shared his memory of stage fright with me. What he experienced as a child is very much related to all of us.

I was an altar boy at the Catholic Church in my neighborhood when I was 12 years old. I was informed in March that I had been chosen as one of the altar boys for the Easter morning High Mass, which was a tremendous honor. I was both delighted and frightened since I knew that most of my friends would see me up there. As the day approached, I had a growing sense of dread, fearful that I would make some foolish blunder that would make all of my friends laugh at me. I awakened early on Easter Sunday morning, filled with worry. I went to the bathroom and puked. I left home without breakfast and strolled to St. Thomas' Church.

I was confident that the inmates on death row, walking to their executions, felt no worse than I did. I splashed water on my face in front of a basin in the altar boys' room, hoping for a last-minute relief – maybe the mass would be canceled, possibly there'd be a fire alarm, maybe, just perhaps the anxiety would go away. It didn't work out. Finally, it was 11 p.m., and the window of opportunity for a miracle had gone. I followed the three priests celebrating the huge mass out to the church's sacristy with the other altar boys. I took a peek across the assembly and noticed some of my acquaintances among the crowd. The cathedral was hot, and the stiff collar I was wearing was tightening by the minute.

Then something occurred. The dazzling lights faded, the altar appeared to rise, and I passed out.

My male friends teased me about the incident, but nothing could compare to the humiliation I felt. It was so severe that I couldn't stomach speaking in class for several years, and I pretended to be sick anytime I had to give a presentation. I became disgruntled with myself, despising my unmanly lack of self-assurance. Finally, in ninth grade, I was nominated for class president, and despite my apprehensions, I campaigned for and won the position. Being president also entailed serving as the school's emcee. The first time I had to do it, it was a nightmare, but I managed to get through it. The following several assemblies were much better. To my amazement, I was beginning to like my new role, and after all of the terrors, it was a welcome change.

The glee club was scheduled to perform various motivating songs during the school's last assembly of the year. I'd become so confident that I memorized the choices, composers, dates, and other details I'd be announcing so I wouldn't have to read them off a card. Obviously, I was bragging, but it was such a thrilling sensation, especially in comparison to my Easter Sunday experience.

Just in case, I placed a card with the information written on it beneath my chair. Everything was OK until the sixth song. I was standing in front of the microphone, ready to announce it, when I realized I couldn't recall any of the facts.

I'm sure it wasn't more than 30 seconds, but the anxious stillness seemed to stretch an hour.

Thankfully, the title of the pick came to me, and I declared it in a weak voice, omitting the other lost information. Before the last two options, I snuck the card out from beneath my seat and quickly looked at the news.

Five teachers approached me after the assembly. I thought to myself, "Boy, I'm in for it now," but they patted me on the back and congratulated me. "Thank you very much," I answered, grinning as if I understood what was going on. "We're so proud of you," one of them exclaimed. "You're the first president we can recall who had the courage and ability to wait until the kids had quieted down before speaking!"

I couldn't possibly lose! "Wow, this phobia is defeated," I thought. It wasn't the case. Throughout the years that followed, I was a nervous speaker on several occasions. However, this early triumph demonstrated that progress is feasible. We can only progress if we thrust our necks out like the turtle.

One of the most frequent anxiety disorders is social phobia, which is described in this autobiographical story. It's called a condition since Peter didn't simply experience stage fright; he couldn't speak in front of a group for years. The word "disorder" can have a negative connotation, even indicating mental illness.

However, psychologists simply refer to situations that significantly disrupt normal behavior and last more than a few weeks.

We feel you must understand the eight various forms of anxiety disorders. You will be better able to communicate with professionals and other parents about your child's condition. Many phrases in psychology are misconstrued (for example, many individuals use the term "paranoid," which refers to a severe form of schizophrenia when they actually mean "suspicious"). It will benefit you in a variety of ways if you understand and utilize these phrases correctly. Knowing more explicitly if your child has one of these conditions may reduce some of your own concerns (only a professional can tell you for sure).

CHAPTER 3: THE EIGHT TYPES OF ANXIETIES

Many children suffer from separation anxiety. Therefore, they avoid going to school or to social gatherings. Knowing something about this condition is helpful. It might make it easier for you to implement each of the COPE steps:

1. Calm the nerves – create a visualization system.
2. Come up with a creative approach – you may assist your child in coming up with a unique technique to record his/her feelings regularly that he/she will genuinely utilize.
3. Stick with it - you may add extra "private time" to his/her incentive structure.
4. Evaluate - you might want to assist your child in keeping track of his /her "resistance to leaving home" ratings (the lower the resistance, the lower the separation anxiety).

We'll go through the eight primary types of anxiety disorders in this chapter:

- Specific (simple) phobia.
- Social phobia.
- Separation anxiety.
- Generalized anxiety disorder (GAD).
- Panic disorder.
- Agoraphobia.

- Obsessive-compulsive disorder (OCD).
- Post-traumatic stress disorder (PTSD).

Children and teenagers might suffer from any of these anxiety disorders. More than one of these conditions may manifest simultaneously, making it difficult to pinpoint a single cause.

Specific (Simple) Phobia

A specific phobia is an exaggerated fear of a situation or thing that poses a minimal risk in reality.

Animal phobias (animals or insects), natural environment phobias (thunder, wind, heights, and so on), blood injection injury phobias (seeing blood, receiving a shot, and so on), situational phobias (flying, tunnels, bridges, and so on), and others are only a few examples.

These phobias, expected in early childhood, are usually not debilitating and go away as the child grows older. However, in the case of some children and adolescents, specific phobias that are not overcome can be debilitating. Specific phobias might become ingrained in a child's everyday life if they feel compelled to avoid items that cause them anxiety. For the child and their family, this can be a cause of great stress and anguish.

Another factor to examine when determining if a child has a phobia is whether a specific phobia has evolved as a secondary problem due to trauma. Take, for example, a child who has had a catastrophic injury in a vehicle accident and has developed a fear of driving. Another example is a child who has been bitten by a dog and has developed a fear of animals.

Social Phobia

If a child or teenager develops several phobias, he may grow so humiliated by them that he refuses to be exposed in public. He is constantly worried about shame because he believes he will do poorly, especially if one of his phobias flares up.

If he goes on a picnic, for example, his enemy, a dog, may come, and his anxiety will be mocked. Some social settings might be more stressful than others. For instance, he may have no difficulty asking a teacher for directions yet be scared to speak in front of his class.

Unfortunately, some young children shut themselves off of the social world vocally. This is known as "selective mutism," a sign of social anxiety. In specific social contexts, the child cannot communicate, while they can communicate well with others. Selective mutism commonly begins in childhood and can last throughout puberty if left untreated.

Separation Anxiety

Separation anxiety is particularly prevalent among children and early teenagers. When a child is away from familiar people and environments, this happens. An individual with a separation anxiety disorder may have significant anxiety (lasting at least four weeks) following normal separation from parents, other caregivers, home, and other familiar surroundings.

Younger children with separation anxiety frequently cry, cling, and panic when separated. Separation anxiety disorder in older children manifest in unrealistic worries about potential damage to loved ones or fears that they will not come home, a reluctance to sleep alone, refusal to attend school, and physical symptoms such as a stomach-ache or headache.

Generalized Anxiety Disorder

In a wide range of settings, young individuals with a generalized anxiety disorder (GAD) show excessive or exaggerated concern. They may spend more time than necessary focusing on the intricacies of activities such as schoolwork or other routine duties. Children with GAD may also exhibit any of the physical symptoms listed below:

- Restlessness.
- Tiredness.

- Inability to concentrate.
- Irritability.
- Unusual muscle tightness.
- Sleep disturbances.

A child with GAD can be said to "fear being fearful." He generates increased worry when he is presented with the likelihood of being in an uncomfortable position because he perceives himself as someone who cannot manage stress effectively.

Panic Disorder

Panic disorder affects children and teenagers, causing them to feel recurring and sudden terror. These episodes are known as "panic attacks" and cause a lot of discomfort and disturbance. Although panic disorder is uncommon in early childhood, it becomes more prevalent in older children and teenagers, most likely due to hormonal factors.

Agoraphobia

When a child's anxiety is so extreme that they cannot engage in most social situations, agoraphobia is diagnosed instead of social phobia. The term stems from roughly 2,500year-old mythology. Panic episodes are nearly always associated with agoraphobia, although they can also affect non-agoraphobics. Panic episodes can also increase agoraphobics' anxiety by making them worry about what might happen if they have a panic attack.

Agoraphobics may also be concerned about being in a situation where aid may be unavailable, such as in the middle of a wide bridge amid a traffic jam.

Hallway Panic (MDM)

One of my friends, Alfred, spoke about his nine-year-old daughter Sarah, who suffers from panic attacks:

Sarah is apprehensive on her way to school and starts biting her nails. Her heart starts to pound as soon as she comes through the main entrance of her school. Her chest feels like it's about to explode with each step Sarah takes, and Sarah's afraid. All she can do is remain there and beg for rescue with her wet eyes.

A teacher from across the hall observes her worry and goes over to inquire about it. Sarah wishes she could tell him anything, but all she can do is cry and sob.

This is a classic case of hallway anxiety.

Obsessive-Compulsive Disorder (OCD)

Children with OCD are bothered by recurrent and persistent thoughts – "obsessions" – that take up more than one hour of their time each day and are usually associated with heightened worry. To relax or vent the stress generated by their obsessive thoughts, these children feel forced to engage in repetitive actions known as "compulsions."

Young children with OCD are particularly prone to compulsions such as collecting every stone on the beach, preserving candy wrappers, washing, counting, praying, and hoarding compulsively. The problem is usually not the act itself, but it is how often the child feels compelled to execute it.

Post-traumatic stress disorder (PTSD)

Post-traumatic stress disorder (PTSD) is a severe condition with a wide range of potentially deadly consequences. Any child suspected of suffering from PTSD must receive expert help as soon as possible. It ranges from minor issues to life-threatening conditions, and only an expert can determine the difference.

The symptoms of PTSD in children and adolescents can manifest in various ways, but there are a few things to look out for. The traumatic event may be relived in the form of thoughts or feelings for a long time. Children may engage in play behaviors that reflect themes or parts of the initial traumatic event. Other signs and symptoms include:

- Recurrent, distressing memories of the traumatic event.
- Upsetting dreams about the traumatic event.
- Reluctance to think or talk about the traumatic event.
- Avoiding places, activities, or people that remind you of the event.
- Inability to experience positive emotions.
- Hopelessness about the future.

• Trouble sleeping.

We understand that learning about these eight anxiety disorders has most likely made you feel anxious. It's similar to the "medical student syndrome," in which students believe they have whatever illness they're studying. Parents may think that their child exhibits any of the symptoms listed in this chapter after reading about anxiety symptoms.

However, understanding the differences between the eight categories is vital to engage in your child's rehabilitation properly. The good news is that practically every child with one of these disorders can be significantly helped.

If you believe your child may have agoraphobia, panic disorder, OCD, or PTSD, I recommend that you get help from a qualified therapist or psychiatrist.

You can help your child with most of the suggestions in this book, but if the problem does not go away in a fair amount of time, you should seek expert help. For the most part, the therapist will be delighted to work with you in using this book to assist your child.

CHAPTER 4: LEARNING TO THINK REALISTICALLY

Learning to think more realistically is a powerful method for overcoming anxiety in anyone, adult or child. As part of your child's program, it will be especially beneficial. Even for adults, though, it is a complex technique to master. As a result, learning to employ this ability yourself is the best way to assist your child in using it properly. As a result, we've divided this chapter into two sections. In the first section, I will teach you the concepts and methods of realistic thinking to fully comprehend how it works by putting it into practice. This way, you will understand how it functions.

In the second part of the chapter, I will show you how to teach realistic thinking to your child, calling it "detective thinking" and making it a little easier to understand than the entire technique you'll be employing.

The Fundamentals of Realistic Thinking

There are several basic principles that you must understand before you can learn to adjust your ideas and, as a result, manage your feelings and aid your child.

The Interaction between Events, Thoughts, and Feelings

The majority of people believe that feelings are caused by circumstances that occur outside of their control. In other words, if you go through a given incident, you will undoubtedly have certain feelings. How often have you stated something like "You made me so angry" or "That loudness scared me"? However, outside occurrences, such as traffic delays or another person's conduct, cannot be held entirely accountable for your emotions. One way to grasp this is to realize that two people can have the same experience yet have different reactions. The same person can have multiple experiences with the same event and have very different feelings about it each time. What is the reason for this?

The solution is found in the substance of your beliefs, thoughts, or self-talk—in other words, your sentiments are influenced by what you tell yourself about a situation.

Assume Tony's and Jim's wives are both an hour late getting home from the movies. Tony convinces himself that his wife most likely went out for coffee with a friend (his belief about the situation). He is unconcerned about her due to his belief, yet he is irritated that she didn't think to call and let him know. On the other hand, Jim convinces himself that his wife was killed in a vehicle accident (this is his belief about the situation). He is worried sick as a result of harboring this belief.

This example clearly indicates that the feelings experienced by each man are not caused by the scenario (wife being late). Instead, each person's views or thoughts are to blame for their various reactions. The incident may serve as a trigger. However, the feeling generated by the catalyst is determined by how the person interprets the event.

Although it is easy to believe that how we react to an event is determined by the event itself, our beliefs and thoughts based on our interpretations of the experience directly impact how we respond. Keep in mind that our emotions aren't directly influenced by what's going on in our environment. This is an important consideration as you and your child progress through this book. On the other hand, our feelings and emotions directly result from how we think about and interpret events and situations.

Two Common Thinking Mistakes

Most people who are worried or stressed make two errors in their thinking. For starters, people frequently overestimate the likelihood of unpleasant things happening. Second, people often anticipate that the events' results or effects would be disastrous and terrible.

1. Overestimating Probability

An anxious person frequently feels that unpleasant things are almost certain to happen to them, even if this is not the case. Consider someone who is really nervous having to stand up and deliver a speech at a wedding.

"I simply know I'm going to say the wrong thing," they could think. It's conceivable that this individual will now say something that isn't quite acceptable. But it's challenging to say the wrong thing at a wedding, and the chances of that individual saying the incorrect thing is little to none. When you say to yourself, "I'm going to say the incorrect thing," you're implying that you'll indeed say the wrong thing. Clearly, this is an exaggeration.

Similarly, if you arrive late, your child may get concerned if they assume "Mom and Dad have been in an accident." However, this assumption suggests a 100 percent certainty—"Mom and Dad have unquestionably been in an accident." While there's a potential you've been in an accident, the fact is that it's scarce. If your child believes it is inevitable, this is an exaggeration that will just add to their anxiety.

2. Overestimating Consequences

Life might appear quite scary to persons who are excessively stressed. Not only do they feel that bad things will almost certainly happen to them, but they also believe that if they do, the repercussions will be catastrophic and terrible.

Surprisingly, most people who assume the worst are entirely unconscious of their actions. To put it another way, they have rarely asked themselves, "What is the worst thing that might happen, and could I deal with it if it did?"

Consider the following scenario: you're driving to an appointment. "Oh my, I'm going to be extremely late," you say to yourself as you are stuck in traffic while driving your car. You assume that being late will be extremely unpleasant as a result of this idea. To put it another way, you're telling yourself, "I'm going to be late, and that's going to be the end of the world." However, if you ask yourself, "What will actually happen if I am late, and will I be able to cope with it?" you will likely discover that being late is not as dreadful as you might have thought.

Consider this scenario: your child is really concerned about making a mistake in their homework. They are undoubtedly afraid of making a mistake since it will be the "end of the world." In reality, while the teacher may remark about it, making a mistake on a piece of homework is unlikely to have any long-term consequences. This demonstrates the second sort of systematic thinking error: exaggerating the negative repercussions of events.

Activity for Parents- Finding Proof of My Own Concern

This is not a simple skill to learn, whether for adults or children. Try to learn the skill for yourself before moving on to teaching it to your child.

Consider a recent occurrence that led you to be concerned.

What were your feelings or beliefs regarding the incident?

_____
_____
_____
_____

What level of concern did you have? (Use the scale of 0 to 10 to measure your level of anxiety.)

0 _____ 10

What has happened in the past when you've had a similar concerning thought?

_____
_____
_____

What information about this event is available?

_____
_____
_____
_____

What other possible explanation do you have?

_____
_____
_____
_____

What would you believe if you were in someone else's shoes?

_____
_____
_____
_____

What would it mean if what you believe came true?

_____
_____
_____
_____

What would have been a reasonable belief to hold given all of the evidence?

_____
_____
_____
_____

How concerned do you think you would have been if you had believed this instead? (Use the scale of 0 to 10 to measure your level of anxiety.)

0   10
_____

Teaching Your Child About Realistic Thinking

We've discussed challenging things to grasp. Applying these principles to your own thoughts and beliefs is much more difficult. It's understandable to be concerned about how you'll convey these concepts to your child. In a nutshell, you will teach a reduced version of these ideas to your child. Your child will need to practice realistic thinking regularly by utilizing the Detective Thinking Worksheet, which we'll show you later in the section "An Example of Detective Thinking" below. This worksheet is highly similar to the above-mentioned Realistic Thinking Worksheet, which you should have tried out.

By the end of this chapter, your child should have a firm grasp of numerous vital concepts. These points will be made in the tasks and readings you and your kid will do together. It's also critical to underline and reemphasize these themes as much as possible. The following are the main points:

• Thoughts are what we say to ourselves; they are significant because they influence our moods and behavior.

• Being a good detective and seeking objective evidence may frequently turn worried thoughts into peaceful ideas.

The content you'll be going through with your child in this chapter is divided into three phases. Each of which builds on the one before it. The first level is assisting your child in understanding what thoughts are and developing skills in identifying their own ideas, which you began in the previous chapter. The second level involves helping your child understand why thoughts are essential. The third stage consists of acting as a detective and evaluating the facts to assist your child in countering anxious thoughts. In the following parts, I'll give you some directions for explaining these concepts to your child, and after the chapter, I'll provide you with some exercises to help your child grasp the concepts.

Why Are Thoughts Important?

The children's activities after the chapter will assist you in briefly explaining the basic concept of realistic thinking to your child, just as we discussed at the beginning of this chapter. Obviously, depending on your child's age, this will need a more basic version than previously explained. It is critical to highlight the importance of thinking with your child, ensuring that they know that more than one idea is available in any given scenario and that their thoughts will affect how they feel. As a result, if children alter their thinking, they may change their feelings as well.

The Detective Approach

As we described earlier, one of the most typical errors that nervous children make in their thinking is to overestimate the likelihood that terrible or hazardous things will happen to them.

As a result, anxious children must learn to assess the possibility of their negative, anxious perceptions of something being true or correct. This will assist them in believing in their peaceful ideas.

Your child will need to learn to uncover evidence for their unfavorable expectations in the same way you evaluate your negative beliefs. It's critical that your children, like you, believe in their calm minds. You mustn't just tell your child that a frightening notion is ridiculous or unrealistic, as they are unlikely to trust you and will likely get even more disturbed. Instead, your child must realize that their perception is doubtful due to the evidence collecting procedure.

Three steps make up the overall strategy.

1. The first stage is for children to figure out what is bothering them. They must recognize their anxious mindset. Remind your child of the distinction between feelings and thinking. It's preferable if your child's frightening thought is a clear description of what they anticipate about the happening. "I am afraid that Dad was murdered in a vehicle accident," for example, is an excellent, unambiguous statement that your

child may utilize with their detective thinking. A notion like "I'm terrified because Dad isn't here," on the other hand, doesn't explain what your child is actually afraid of and hence cannot be readily worked with.

2. The second step is for your child to gather as many clues as possible about the worrying thought. This is where your child gets to play detective and try to work out how they might really "know" whether the thing they are afraid of will really happen. The most accessible types of evidence to find may include the following:

- What has happened in this case before?
- What do I know about this circumstance in general?
- Is there anything more that may occur in this situation?
- Which scenario is most likely to occur?
- What has happened to the rest of the group?

We don't ask children to consider the repercussions ("What if that happened?"). Children, particularly younger ones, have a hard time with this. You might be able to ask them about the probable implications yourself at times. However, it is preferable to have children focus on evidence to demonstrate that what they are afraid of is unlikely to occur in most circumstances.

1. Finally, children will be able to do the third step—re-evaluating their frightening thought—based on the evidence

they have considered. Hopefully, they will see that the frightened thinking is unlikely and that a more likely calm notion is the better way forward. Remember, this is a practical thinking exercise, not a positive thinking activity. This implies that there will be times when anxious thinking will be the more likely option. Consider a child who ventures out after dark and finds themselves in a dark alley where they witness someone breaking into a house. It is critical to tell children that feeling scared in such situations is completely natural and beneficial. The detective thinking that you are teaching your child is intended to assist your child in replacing anxious ideas with calm thoughts when their anxieties are excessive and unreasonable. It is not intended to be used in all situations.

How to Teach Your Child Detective Thinking

You've realized that some thoughts are counterproductive. They make you feel anxious and afraid, and they might influence you to do things that will harm you. Fortunately, there are several things you may do to combat your anxious thoughts.

The initial step is to seize them. This is something you've done before. When you see yourself becoming concerned, terrified, or apprehensive, the first thing you should do is identify the troubling thought that is causing you to feel this way.

Then, next to the "What am I worried about" heading on the Detective Thinking Worksheet, write it down. You may also use the worry scale to determine the severity of your anxiety.

The next stage is to transform into a detective and search for any traces of your frightening idea. A detective's task is to search for evidence and clues to discover the truth. This is what you must do as well. "How do I know whether it's actually true?" you should ask yourself when you examine your frightening thought. Then you'll need to hunt for clues to see if your frightened thinking is correct. Here are some questions to ask yourself to ensure that you consider all of the facts. (You may point these out to your child on the Detective Thinking Worksheet, or you can write them out on cards to stimulate them while learning the skill.)

What has happened in this case before?

_____
_____
_____
_____

Have you ever been in a similar situation?

_____
_____
_____
_____

Is there anything awful that occurred?

_____
_____
_____
_____

When you were in the scenario, did something unpleasant happen every time?

_____
_____
_____
_____

Do you have any broad background knowledge about this situation?

___

Is this a genuinely dire situation?

___

Have any of your friends or acquaintances experienced something similar?

___

Is there anything more that may happen in this situation?

_____
_____
_____
_____

Could there be another explanation for this?

_____
_____
_____
_____

Is it possible that anything else will occur?

_____
_____
_____
_____

After you've gathered your proof, the last step is to consider it all and determine how much you believe in your frightened notion (based on the evidence). "Based on my clues, what do I actually think will happen?" is the question you ask yourself. "Can I come up with an alternative, more peaceful thought?" On the last line of the Detective Thinking Worksheet, write your calm thinking. Finally, consider how frightened you would be if you genuinely believed your new clear review. Make a note of the number on the concern scale.

A Final Point to Consider

You and your child should avoid being overly perfectionistic when you both are learning this skill. The idea is, your kids must learn to replace anxious thoughts with more realistic and peaceful ones and believe them. At this phase, it is less crucial how these thoughts arrive, and they may differ slightly from case to case. Some children, especially those who are very young, may not be able to collect evidence in the manner that we have advised. However, if they practice coming up with calm, realistic thoughts, they may be able to think more calmly. For some children who have a hard time learning to gather evidence (e.g., more concrete thinkers), just learning to recognize their own worried thinking and then attempting to anticipate a calm idea will help them feel less anxious. If your child is having trouble grasping the detective thinking principles, go to the self-talk activity in this chapter, where two persons had opposing viewpoints on the same subject.

Then just return to having your youngster bring up a calm idea whenever they feel fearful or concerned. "What would Jessica think if her mommy was late picking her up from school?" is a good example of how to fantasize about a superhero as a replacement for Jessica's mother. Obviously, employing the entire detective thought process is preferable. However, for some children, merely learning to think of a calm idea when they are afraid will help to alleviate their dread.

Finally, keep in mind that this isn't the sole method for dealing with worry. If your child still can't grasp detective thinking (despite a valiant effort), you may wish to move on to some of the other strategies guided by a professional therapist.

Why are thoughts important?

Explain to your child that every circumstance is made up of a series of events, thoughts, feelings, and actions. Emphasize that the same scenario can result in two different ideas and that these thoughts lead to different feelings and behaviors. To support your argument, use the example below or something similar.

Point out that altering an emotion requires first changing an idea, as the thought comes first. Emphasize that we all have peaceful thoughts that make us feel good and motivate us to do good things. Other times, we experience anxious thoughts that make us feel horrible and cause us to do things that aren't beneficial.

Ask your child to determine which of Harry's and Mike's views were helpful and why:

Harry's Story

Harry is at the cinema with his family when he notices a classmate on the other side of the hall just before the movie begins. Harry greets his pal with a wave and a kind greeting.

The companion remains silent. "He must not have heard me." Harry thinks to himself. "After the movie, I'll go over to where he's sitting and say hi to him." Harry is in good spirits. He sits silently in his seat, engrossed in the film. When it's completed, he walks over to his friend's seat on the opposite side of the cinema and greets him. His friend is delighted to see Harry, and the two decide to play the next day.

Mike's Story

Mike is also at the cinema with his family. He notices a classmate on the other side of the room just before the movie begins. Mike gives a friendly wave to his pal. The companion remains silent. "Oh, he ignored me," Mike thinks to himself. "He must despise me. Everyone could see that he was ignoring me. I can't believe this happened to me. I'm such a loser." Mike is ashamed and depressed. He doesn't seem to enjoy the film since he's preoccupied with what happened before the movie. Mike avoids his pal when he meets him at school on Monday.

Self-Talk

This game is intended to help your child grasp the concept that a person may think in a variety of ways in the same scenario and that these diverse ideas will result in a variety of feelings and behaviors. Look for photographs or cartoons showing a child in scenarios like confronting a large dog, meeting a new child, delivering a speech, or waiting for someone to return home.

Have your child create two possible ideas that the child in the photo may be thinking of using the pictures. Encourage your youngster to distinguish between calm and troubled thinking. Then, use a table with the column headings:

Thought

_____

Feeling

_____

Behavior

_____

Ask your child to fill in the blanks for a calm response and a worried response to situations like
- "I haven't finished my homework."
- "I want to invite a new friend to my house."

- "My team has a semi-final tomorrow."
- "Summer camp begins on Monday."

Ask your child these questions:

- What is the lasting impression of thought on you?
- How do you feel after having the thought?
- What have you decided to do in response to this thought?

Use detective thinking for bigger issues

The information you read earlier about teaching detective thinking has a lesson for every parent. Children who worry a lot tend to believe that bad things happen a lot or that it will be a disaster if something bad does happen. They often think that one way to feel less worried is to figure out if the worrying thought is realistic or not. Explain to your child that you may accomplish this by searching for "clues." This way, your child can find whether or not a worrisome idea is true.

Follow these steps to think more realistically:

- Make a list of the occurrence, your thoughts, and how worried you are on a scale of one to ten.
- To assist you in uncovering the proof, ask yourself questions like "What are the facts?" and "What is likely to happen or has happened previously with you or other people?"

- Make a list of everything that may go wrong in the given circumstance.
- Using the hints, generate a realistic notion and assess how concerned you would be if you had it instead of a worrying thought.

To demonstrate how detective thinking works, read through one or two of the examples provided earlier in the chapter. Completing the examples is the greatest way to show your child how to apply detective thinking in real-life scenarios.

Help them uncover proof of realistic ideas for two basic scenarios: "A huge dog is approaching me," and the following thinking, "The dog is going to attack me, and I won't be able to stop him," or "There's a weird noise outside," and the thought, "A robber is attempting to break in."

Try it for more complicated issues after your children have practiced detective thinking on their minor issues for at least one week. Once your children grasp the concept, assist them in completing the detective thinking worksheets for more serious concerns, attempting to cover at least two scenarios. Remember to ask your children the questions given above to assist them in gathering the best evidence for each case. Allow your child to "coach" you on one of your own concerns if you are having difficulties. Allow your child to ask you the questions and assist you in generating proof for your concern, as well as a calm, realistic idea. When the matter is not personal, it is generally simpler to practice.

Detective thinking is a difficult skill to master. However, it can assist anxious children in calming their nerves when they perceive an unrealistic threat. Every time children feel uncomfortable, bashful, scared, or terrified. They should fill out a detective thinking worksheet. The more they practice, the better they'll grow at it, and the more likely they'll use detective thinking when they're truly nervous.

To begin, you'll almost certainly need to be heavily involved and assist your child. You can gradually reduce the assistance as soon as they are showing improvements. Older children may be able to take up the skills in a matter of days, while younger children may require assistance for several weeks.

Sit down with your child and talk about the day, using detective thinking to look for any negative experiences or anxieties. Even practicing them after the incident is beneficial. Obviously, the idea is to make your child think like a detective in a scary circumstance. As a result, anytime you detect your children becoming agitated, encourage them to apply this technique. You will need to prompt in detail early on in the process, assisting your child with the particular stages and questions. This means that you will need to memorize the method and prepare some evidence-gathering questions that are relevant to a specific scenario.

CHAPTER 5: DIFFERENT PROFESSIONALS, ONE GOAL

Many people work to assist children with emotional issues. Even though they have various names and credentials, you'll discover that their similarities outnumber their differences:

Psychologists

Anyone can call oneself a psychologist at the moment, which is a bit of an issue. You should be alright if you take your child to visit a psychologist at the NHS since their credentials should have been examined. However, if you're going to see someone secretly, be cautious. Whether you want to be sure you're receiving someone with the proper credentials, ask if they're 'chartered.' This indicates that the British Psychological Society has reviewed and validated their certificates (BPS). You can visit the BPS website if you have any questions.

Clinical psychologists, counseling psychologists, and educational psychologists are the three types of psychologists your child might consult.

Clinical Psychologist

A clinical psychologist will typically have a psychology degree, job experience, and a three-year postgraduate degree. The title "Dr." is used by the majority of clinical psychologists, although not all.

They'll have received specialized training in working with kids and teenagers.

Counseling Psychologist

A counseling psychologist will have a bachelor's degree in psychology and at least one year of postgraduate study. Some counseling psychologists are also known as "Dr." Psychologists, on the other hand, are not medically trained. They do not prescribe medications in this country, at least for the time being.

You can be directed to a "trainee" counselor or clinical psychologist as well. These individuals have a psychology degree and are pursuing chartered counseling or clinical psychologist certification. Even if they are not certified, they should be supervised by an experienced supervisor who regularly supervises their performance. You should not be afraid to see them; typically, the most junior staff members are updated with the latest research.

Educational Psychologist

Educational psychologists may also be found. Educational psychologists generally work in schools, so your child may be sent to an educational psychologist if he has academic problems. These experts have a psychology degree as well as a teaching certificate. Before pursuing a one-year professional certificate in school psychology, they will have taught for some time.

They mainly help students who are struggling academically at school or who are experiencing behavioral issues at school. They may conduct some one-on-one work with a child, but their primary responsibility is to assist the school in providing the most excellent possible assistance for the child.

Psychiatrists

Psychiatrists are medical specialists who specialize in mental health issues. They will have specialization in mental health after four to six years of medical school and an additional year of general training. Psychiatrists have a variety of titles that indicate their level of experience. A 'Registrar' is a relatively junior psychiatrist whose work will be tightly monitored by a more senior psychiatrist. A 'Specialist Registrar,' or 'SPR,' is a higher-ranking employee who, although being nearly wholly trained, will have their work overseen by a consultant. The most senior psychiatrist is known as a 'Consultant.' At the present, a psychiatrist is the only doctor you're likely to visit who can give your child medicine. Your GP or, in rare cases, a paediatrician are the sole exceptions.

Counselors and Therapists

Anyone may call themselves a counselor or a therapist. You may encounter a range of counselors/therapists, from those with little training and experience to highly trained and talented experts. If you find a counselor/therapist through your doctor or a hospital, you may be confident that they have completed some form of training.

If you decide to take your child to a private therapist, be highly selective about who you choose. At the absolute least, be sure that your therapist is a member of the UKCP.

CAMHS Workers and Primary Mental Health Workers

You may be given an appointment with a 'Child and Adolescent Mental Health (CAMHS) Worker or a Primary Mental Health Worker if you are referred to a hospital or clinic. These individuals have a range of backgrounds, the most common of which being social work and nursing. They have decided to focus on children's mental health and have obtained specialized training in this area.

Psychiatric Nurses

You may be offered an appointment with a psychiatric nurse if you are referred to a hospital. Psychiatric nurses have often received one of two types of education. Many of them began their careers as general nurses who dealt with physical health issues before pursuing more education and specializing in mental health.

People have lately been allowed to train specifically as mental health nurses without first completing regular nursing training. Nurses have undergone extensive training in both circumstances, and their work is closely supervised until they gain experience.

CHAPTER 6: WHAT KIND OF THERAPY WILL BE GIVEN TO MY CHILD?

Cognitive Behaviour Therapy

Unfortunately, research into the best therapies for childhood and adolescent anxiety and depression is still in its early phases. 'Cognitive Behaviour Therapy,' or 'CBT,' has been a popular treatment for anxious and depressed people since the 1970s. In a moment, I'll explain what this is all about.

Hundreds of studies have demonstrated that cognitive behavior therapy is helpful for people with a variety of anxiety and depressive disorders. It is probably on par with pharmaceuticals in terms of effectiveness. People have begun to investigate whether CBT is effective for children with anxiety or depression in the last decade or two. The National Institute for Clinical Excellence (NICE) is a British government body that determines the best therapies for various health issues. They compile all of the data, confer with multiple specialists in the field, and prepare a report on the most effective therapies. They decide what the NHS should do. The National Institute for Health and Clinical Excellence (NICE) has published a paper on managing depressive children and teens.

They concluded that if depression is more than a fleeting phase or a reaction to an adverse event (such as bullying), every child should be administered cognitive behavior therapy in the first instance.

The National Institute for Health and Clinical Excellence (NICE) has not yet published a study on child anxiety, although the scientific evidence for anxiety is remarkably comparable to depression. In general, cognitive-behavioral therapy appears to work well for child anxiety. Because there is little evidence that alternative psychological therapies work, cognitive behavior therapy is probably the best course of action.

What is Cognitive Behaviour Therapy?

Cognitive behavior therapy (CBT) tries to assist people in altering their perceptions of themselves and the environment. People who are anxious or depressed, according to current thought, have created a complicated system of beliefs that lead them to believe that the world is hazardous, challenging, and uncontrollable. It's not strange that we feel terrified or unhappy if we consider these things. These sets of beliefs appear to exist in children as well, albeit they appear to be less crystallized than in adults. When we utilize cognitive behavior therapy to modify these beliefs, we know that patients start to feel better. During cognitive behavior therapy, your child will most likely be seen by one therapist who will talk to them about their ideas and feelings about things.

If any of these thoughts drive anxiety or depression, the therapist will work with you and your child to eliminate them. Completing fun worksheets, doing little experiments to see whether their views are actual, and playing games to try out different ways of thinking are all activities that the therapist will urge your child to undertake.

The therapist will frequently ask your child to try different ways of behaving (for example, getting out more) to see whether this improves matters. Although cognitive behavior therapy might lead to challenging topics, the goal with children is to make the sessions as enjoyable as possible. You may also discover that the therapist wants to include you in specific sessions, especially if your child is younger. Your child will normally be given assignments to complete at home to supplement what is being done in the sessions. The therapist may try to enlist your help in ensuring that these tasks are complete.

Although the therapist will want to chat to you about supporting your child without feeling invasive, your help can make a massive difference between success and failure. The therapist will usually offer you six sessions, to begin with. Following that, you, your child, and the therapist will meet to discuss the situation and determine whether anything further needs to be done or whether additional sessions are necessary. Unless the problem is challenging, treatment rarely lasts more than twenty sessions if you stick to it.

Interpersonal Therapy

Interpersonal therapy is a subset of CBT. It has been reported to be effective in some cases of depression where the issue appears to be forming relationships with others. In this country, it is not extensively utilized. However, if cognitive behavior therapy does not work for your child, it may be worth looking for someone specializing in this form of therapy, as NICE suggests.

Family therapy

As I mentioned before, we don't have a lot of research on what works for children's anxiety and depression. Only a few studies have been done to see if family therapy may help with these issues. However, many well-respected psychologists and psychiatrists swear by it, and just because no one has shown that it works does not indicate that it does not. If you're concerned about any of your family's relationships, family therapy may be an excellent option. If you are invited to participate in family therapy, you may expect to accompany your spouse. You will also need to accompany all of your children.

Other key family members (for example, grandparents) may be invited as well. Family therapy aims to modify how family members interact with and feel about one another to create a calmer and more harmonious family life. You might be startled to learn that you have more than one therapist. Some therapists are often not there in the room with you but are observing from behind a screen.

Counseling

Again, we don't know if simply receiving "counseling" is sufficient to assist an anxious or depressed child. We just haven't done the necessary research. If your child is offered to counsel, it's certainly worth a shot, but if things don't improve in a few weeks, it's time to look for other options.

Psychodynamic therapies

Psychodynamic therapies have been tested on adults, although the evidence is inconclusive. Psychodynamic treatments come in a variety of shapes and sizes, which I won't go into here. Today, many individuals believe that these therapies are outdated and based on obsolete notions, such as those proposed by Freud and Jung, rather than contemporary scientific views of what is going on in the depressed or anxious mind. Traditional psychodynamic therapy has been a long-term treatment, with weekly (or even more frequent) sessions lasting from a few months to several years.

Shorter versions of psychodynamic psychotherapy have lately been created, with weekly sessions lasting six months or fewer. Because there is limited evidence that psychodynamic therapy effectively treats depression, NICE recommends that it be used only as a last resort after all other options have been exhausted. If you are given this therapy, it may be worth giving it a try, but if you do not notice any progress after a few weeks, or if you or your child are uncomfortable with it, it may be worth seeking out other help.

Support groups and self-help

There is a lot that parents and carers can do to help themselves and their children, in addition to seeking professional help. This book contains some advice. In addition, seeking out the help of others in a similar situation can be really beneficial.

CHAPTER 7: STRATEGIES FOR PARENTS

There are several approaches to dealing with a child's anxiety; reassuring a child, telling a child exactly how to handle the situation. You can also try empathizing with a child's anxiety by discussing in detail what makes your child anxious and afraid. Sometimes parents try being harsh with a child by not allowing them to avoid the situation, removing a child from the feared situation, or allowing a child to prevent the problem. You'll probably discover that you employ a combination of these tactics at different times, with varying degrees of effectiveness. Some of these tactics are often beneficial in reducing child anxiety, while others are not. Each technique will be examined in further depth.

There is no one-size-fits-all approach to parenting a child, and each child and family is unique. However, there are certain things that parents can do to minimize their child's anxiety in the long run. On the other hand, parents and children might occasionally get into a routine that isn't very useful in dealing with a child's anxiety. Hopefully, this chapter will assist you in gaining objectivity while considering the ways you are presently employing to deal with your child's fear.

Dealing with Anxiety in Children in Unhelpful Ways

While it is true that there are no wrong ways to treat a child, parents can occasionally react to their child's worry in ways that serve to maintain or even worsen the anxiety in the long run.

Reassuring Your Child Too Much

A normal parental response to a child's distress is reassurance. Regrettably, reassurance has little effect on an anxious child, much like water off a duck's back. More significantly, while reassurance may temporarily alleviate your child's worry, the more comfort you provide as a parent, the more reassurance your child will seek in the long term.

What matters most is that you consider when you give your child a lot of attention and reassurance. Obviously, you can't provide too much affection and attention to a really wounded child or a child that has been scared by a potentially dangerous scenario. Let's assume your child was crossing the street, and a car came to a screeching halt only inches from his horrified face. In a scenario like this, there's no way to give too many hugs and kisses. However, if your child begins to be afraid at times when the fear is severe, your hugs and kisses will simply send the message that there is something terrible to be scared of.

Reassurance is a type of positive attention that you may give to your child. This implies that you are essentially rewarding the anxiety if you comfort your child when they are frightened. In certain situations, this may make the child's distress seem nearly worthwhile. At the absolute least, it can assist in teaching children that they are unable to function on their own and require your assistance in dealing with challenging situations. As a result, you may find that you need to hold off on your reassurance for your anxious child even longer than you would for a non-anxious child, merely so that your anxious child is forced to learn that they can do things for himself.

When dealing with a child who has been accustomed to receiving a lot of reassurance, you may need to start giving less and less aid over time. If you want to encourage your child to use their own detective thinking instead of relying on you for comfort, you may need to spend some time with them going through detective thinking the first few times. After a short period, you might anticipate your child to conduct more and more detective thinking on their own. If your child comes to you for comfort, you should eventually be able to simply advise them to do their own investigation into the situation.

This process requires parents to stick to their decision despite their child's questions. Children learn that perseverance pays off, so you'll have to outlast their persistence and stick to your plans as a parent.

Being Too Involved and Directive

Some parents will try to take control and lead their children when they are highly nervous. To put it another way, they will either teach their child exactly what to do, they will teach them how to behave and what to say in an anxiety-provoking circumstance, or they will act on their behalf.

Permitting Avoidance

Anxious children tend to avoid participating in a variety of activities. As a parent, it might be challenging to keep pushing your child to face their fears, so you may cave in and let your child avoid them. It's understandable if this happens on occasion. Obviously, your child's anxiety and distress will decrease in the short term, and you will gain popularity by enabling your child to avoid doing things that they do not want to do. Allowing avoidance in your child, on the other hand, might have significant long-term effects if it becomes a habit. Children will not be able to overcome their nervousness as long as they avoid it.

Becoming Impatient with Your Child

As many parents have told us, it's all too easy to grow impatient and frustrated with an anxious child. Nothing you do or say appears to make a difference. It may seem like children are purposefully hanging to their anxieties at times. It often feels as though "they could accomplish it if they only tried harder."

While it's reasonable that you can lose your cool occasionally, being enraged with your child will only make them more fearful and reliant. If you're losing patience, it's a good idea to enlist the support of another person. It can be your partner. You can try to go away from the situation for the time being to collect your thoughts.

Rewarding Brave, Non-anxious Behavior

No matter how worried a child is, they will do terrifying things at times. As a parent, you should be on the lookout for any signs of bravery in your child, no matter how minor, and praise them. This will increase the chances of the boldness occurring again. Consider it like fanning the embers of a fire to help it expand. To begin, you must seek out an example of bravery and make a big deal out of it. You can later reward only the most apparent instances when your child gets less apprehensive. Make sure you don't have unrealistic expectations. Remember that what may appear insignificant to you may be pretty challenging for a frightened child. You must ensure that you are looking for brave actions based on your child's nature, not based on the standards of others. You may assist your child in developing self-confidence and comprehending what they are capable of by pointing to and emphasizing accomplishments.

You may want to encourage your child to try activities that are a bit tough for them in addition to seeking naturally existing bravery. This, too, should be rewarded. Later in the book, we'll go through this method in further depth.

There are two categories of rewards: material and nonmaterial. Material rewards are the ones that come to mind first for most of us. Money, food, stickers, and toys are examples of such items. After the daring deed is recognized, the child is given a prize, such as a tiny toy. Praise, attention, and interest from the parent are examples of non-monetary incentives. Parental attention is a very potent motivator. Most children, especially younger ones, will go to great lengths to get their parents' acceptance and admiration.

It's also critical to mix up your prizes. If your child receives the same incentive over and over, it will rapidly lose its significance. When it comes to employing incentives, there are a few things to keep in mind:

- Rewards must be relevant to the child to be effective. It's pointless to give a child something they dislike as a reward. Discussing the prize is the most straightforward approach to ensure that the child will work for it. Find out what they are most interested in right now.

- Explain to your child exactly what they have to accomplish to receive incentives. It's pointless to give great incentives to children if they believe they were given for no cause. The child must understand why they are receiving the reward and how to obtain it again.

Clear and precise praise is required. You want your child to understand exactly what they did that you like and what you want them to do again in the future. "John, you were able to go into class by yourself with Jim this morning instead of requiring me to accompany you," for example. "I was so proud of you today" is far more beneficial than "You were such a wonderful boy today, John."

- The incentives must be appropriate for the activity, and you must make sure that the child receives a reward that is the right size for the activity's difficulty. Providing merely a modest token or two minutes of your time is not fair if your child is scared of dogs and has just spent the previous half-hour with the neighbor's dog, who they have never approached before. If your child has done something only marginally challenging, on the other hand, rewarding them with a new television will leave you with nowhere to go.

- Most essential, awards must be offered as quickly as possible following the heroic deed and must be delivered if promised. Effective parenting necessitates consistency. Children will rapidly learn not to trust a parent's word if promises are not kept. If you offer a reward to your child, you must follow through. Similarly, the longer the delay between the incident and the tip, the less effective the prize becomes.

If your child accomplishes something daring on Monday and you thank them with a modest token on Saturday, the effect will be lost.

- If you have more children, you may notice that they are resentful of your nervous child's increased attention and incentives. One approach to get around this is implementing a reward system for all of the children. Introduce a chart where each child may receive incentives for various actions, although the awards may change for each child. You may use the prizes for your other children to promote beneficial habits like obedience, cleaning their teeth, tidying their rooms, and so on, or you can use them to create bravery in all of your children if required.

Teaching Your Child About Rewards

We feel it is equally vital for children to understand what incentives are and how to self-reward in the same way we highlight rewards as an essential aspect of parenting management. Although most children have no issue telling you what they would want as a reward, they tend to conceive of incentives in terms of large and little tangible objects rather than the vast range of options available. There are two goals here: first, to obtain a sense of what incentives your child would want to earn during the activity (remember, the prizes must be relevant to your child, not you), and second, to get your child to start rewarding themselves for the work done.

Ignoring Behaviors That You Don't Want

This strategy is diametrically opposed to the one before it. It requires shifting your attention away from your child's anxious behavior and then returning (and praising) once the anxiety has passed. The idea is that if you notice anything you don't like (for example, your child complaining about being sick before school), you should avoid interacting with them for as long as it continues (whining). Naturally, your child must comprehend why you neglect them and what they must do to reclaim your attention. This strategy should be followed up with positive reinforcement for the child's accomplishments (e.g., complaining stops for one minute).

Prompting Your Child to Cope Constructively

It's critical to express your empathy and understanding in a calm and relaxed manner while chatting with your child about the things that make them uneasy. Children must be heard, understood, and supported. Still, it is also critical that they be encouraged to work constructively to solve the cause of their concern rather than dwelling on how horrible they are feeling. When parents use this method, their children are more likely to think for themselves about how to deal with an anxiety-inducing circumstance. This is in stark contrast to parents who advise their children exactly what to do in a stressful scenario.

Modeling Brave, Non-anxious Behavior

Children, especially when they are younger, learn to act by seeing others, most notably their parents. As a result, everything you do or say as a parent has a more significant meaning since you are a role model for your child. And who do you think your child will connect with the most when it comes to anxiety—the calm, comfortable family member or the somewhat apprehensive, concerned one? Anxious children will naturally relate to a parent who, like them, appears to have a few anxieties of their own when it comes to their fears and worries.

The most excellent form is a coping model, demonstrating that they have worries and anxieties and showing how to deal with them constructively. This model is far more effective than one that appears to have no problems. If you fall into this category, you mustn't try to hide your anxieties from your child or act as if you're never afraid. All this accomplishes is to teach your child that being scared is humiliating or "strange." Instead, think of handling your concerns and worries as a joint endeavor that you and your child can do together.

You may begin to use yourself as a model or practice example for your child once you start communicating honestly with them about your own anxieties. You may, for example, engage your child's help in your detective thinking. This is something that kids will like, and it will teach them how to think more realistically.

When we start creating stepladders, you and your child will each have your own stepladders, which you may use to make anxiety management more enjoyable. Your child, for example, can assist you in working on your stepladder and approaching your concerns, which will teach them more about conquering fears.

Of course, for some parents of anxious children, their own worry can be a significant issue. If you suspect you have an anxiety problem and are having problems dealing with it, you should get help from a mental health expert so that you can start modeling more effective coping for your child.

CHAPTER 8: ESSENTIAL THINGS TO KEEP IN MIND WHEN DEALING WITH ANXIOUS CHILDREN

There are several challenges that parents face when it comes to regulating their anxious child's behavior properly. I have listed some solutions for parents raising an anxious child. Although some of these ideas appear to be self-evident, they are often forgotten.

Being Consistent

You must strive to reward (or punish) your child regularly. Children must learn that certain behaviors result in desirable consequences while others result in bad outcomes.

Keeping Your Emotions in Check

All children may be irritating and stressful at times! This is especially true for anxious children. What could be more aggravating than being late for school because your child refuses to wear a uniform because they are afraid to walk into the other room alone? As normal as it is to become angry, keep in mind that you are significantly less successful as a parent when you are very emotional (e.g., furious or nervous) because consistency is more difficult at such times.

Prepare ahead of time for strategies to "time-out" from interactions with your child when such encounters elicit strong emotional reactions in you. Similarly, it is critical to work on your child's anxiety at a pre-determined time when you are calm and comfortable. You should not teach your child new things when they are terrified of leaving the house or when on the run.

Distinguishing Between Anxious and Naughty Behavior

Drawing a line between a child's anxious behaviors and times when a child is simply bad is one of the most common issues parents face. Parents may receive conflicting advice from well-intentioned individuals who feel that all of their child's actions are purely naughty and should be punished. Unfortunately, the two actions might appear quite similar, but the nervous children do not deserve punishment, making it difficult for parents to know what to do.

Three guidelines might assist you in distinguishing between nervous and naughty behavior:

1. Any sort of verbal or physical hostility is not appropriate, even if a child feels nervous at the moment. That implies that swearing, yelling, punching, and throwing things should all result in immediate repercussions. In the real world, these acts are not tolerated just because someone is upset. Therefore, enabling children to act this way without repercussions will harm them in the long term. They must learn to cope correctly with their emotions, even when they are powerful.

2. You must sift through the circumstances to determine whether there is a reason why your child is avoiding a chore. If you've requested your child to brush their teeth and it hasn't happened, take a step back and assess the issue. Assume you know your child is afraid of the dark, and the restroom is located at the end of the corridor with no lights turned on. It's conceivable that your child is avoiding the chore rather than being disobedient in this scenario. If there are no such restrictions and your child is simply addicted to the television, it is most likely disobedience. Turning off the television for 10 minutes might be a good solution.

3. Take note of how regularly your child appears to avoid a scene. For example, if your child claims that they are afraid to go into their room when there is schoolwork to be done but is perfectly content to remain in there for hours at the computer, you may suspect that your child is exaggerating their worries.

A Few Fundamentals That Can Make a Big Difference

In this section, I'll go through a few simple things you can do as a parent to make a genuine impact on your child's mood.

Diet

We all know that what we eat significantly impacts how we feel, and children are not different.

Take a close look at what your child eats and consider whether this is a contributing factor. Of course, having complete control over your child's diet is difficult. You can, however, have some influence over what children consume at home. This will help even if you only make sure they have a nutritious breakfast.

I will discuss some of the dietary issues that are particularly relevant for anxious or depressed children.

Low blood sugar

Do you know how you feel when you're extremely hungry? — exhausted, lazy, unable to cope, unable to think clearly. We've all experienced it, but if you're prone to anxiety or depression, the intensity of these symptoms is ten times worse. When our blood sugar levels are low, we experience these symptoms. It's imperative to prevent your child from experiencing low blood sugar too frequently. Low blood sugar can occur for a variety of reasons. For example, if we haven't eaten in several hours, our blood sugar drops. So, even if your child isn't hungry, you should strive to make sure that they eat regular meals and get a nutritious snack (such as fruit) in between. Your children must try to consume a healthy breakfast.

When our nutrition is not sufficient, we face dramatic changes in blood sugar levels. Even though we have eaten within the past half-hour, we might still have low blood sugar. When we eat improper meals, this happens. When we consume something really sweet, our blood sugar levels rise, and we feel fantastic.

But then our insulin comes in and eats up all of the blood sugar, causing it to plummet to dangerously low levels. We will feel bad, even though we just ate half an hour ago. 'Simple carbs' are the foods that cause this to happen to our blood sugar. Sweets, chocolate bars, and carbonated beverages all contain these simple carbs. Surprisingly, they are also found in certain meals that we consider to be rather healthy, such as potatoes, white pasta, and white bread.

Caffeine

Caffeine use might cause anxiety in sensitive people. Have you ever had a wobbly sensation after drinking too much coffee? It can also make it difficult to get a good night's sleep. Because getting to sleep may be difficult for anxious and depressed children, it's recommended to limit their caffeine intake during the day and keep them away from it for at least three hours before bedtime. Coffee, both instant and ground, has a high amount of caffeine. It's also in tea. However, not as much as it is in the coffee itself. It can also be found in Cola drinks and chocolates.

Sleep

An anxious or sad child's anxiety or depression might be aggravated by being tired. Some even believe that getting enough sleep is the key to overcoming depression. So, if you can get your child into a habit of obtaining enough high-quality sleep, that would be quite beneficial. Because children's sleep requirements differ, it isn't easy to provide standard guidelines.

According to the Sleep Foundation, children aged 5 to 12 years require 9 to 11 hours of sleep every night, while teens require 8 to 9 hours of sleep. This isn't always the case, though. For example, as children approach their adolescent years, they frequently require more sleep than they did when they were younger.

Does my child have adequate rest?

Is it difficult to wake up your youngster in the morning?

Some people take a long time to get up and can't immediately jump out of bed, but if your child is still sleeping ten minutes after you first try to wake them, they may be receiving insufficient sleep.

Is your youngster prone to dozing off during the day?

Is your child sleeping for significant lengths of time on weekends, as if they're making up for a lost time during the week?

Probably, your youngster isn't getting enough sleep if you responded yes to any of these questions. Remember that as children become older, they may require more sleep and may need to go to bed sooner than younger siblings.

Make an effort to establish a decent sleep habit for your child:

1. Allow yourself an hour or two to wind down before going to bed.

This should include things like taking a bath or reading a book.

2. Try to keep your night-time and waking-up times consistent throughout the day. Your child's body will become accustomed to becoming drowsy at a specific hour. On weekends, this can be up to an hour later. Your child's body will get confused if it is later than that.

3. Make your child's room as calm and dark as possible. If they are fearful of the dark, a little nightlight will suffice.

If your child is a light sleeper, though, blackout curtains or blinds might be considered.

Routines

Depressed and anxious children, in particular, benefit from a regular schedule. One of the issues with anxious and depressive children is that they believe the world is unpredictable and that bad things may happen at any time. A consistent daily schedule allows your child to anticipate what will happen next, and so they will remain calm.

A routine ensures that your child is always aware of what will happen next. It also means that kids can gain some independence — for example, if they know that they always have breakfast before getting dressed, they can learn to get dressed after breakfast without having to wait.

Having a routine does not imply that everything is always the same. Every day is precisely the same. That would be bad for children. They must now learn to cope with a small amount of change.If you're not the 'routine' kind or if you have a large family, it's better to attempt to establish a schedule specifically for everyone.

Exercise

Exercise and mental health have recently been the subject of some very fascinating studies. It has been proven that modest exercise is as effective as treating slightly depressed and anxious children. Exercise will not heal those who are more distressed, but it will undoubtedly aid them in their recuperation.

We all know that today's youngsters do not get nearly as much exercise as we did when we were children. This is unfortunate, not just for their bodies but also for their emotional health. Take a close look at your child and keep track of how much activity they get.

Every day, children and teens should engage in at least half an hour of intense physical exercise. In fact, they would be doing a lot more in a healthy society.

If your child doesn't get close to half an hour of exercise every day, they may be left with pent-up energy, which isn't healthy for their mental health. Not all children are enthusiastic exercisers, but if your child has any interest in this area, do everything you can to encourage them.

Even the most resistant children may tolerate some forms of exercise.

CHAPTER 9: THE SEVEN CONFIDENT THOUGHTS

My society's community center usually has a large banner on the wall when parents come to their meetings for families with nervous or sad children. 'The Seven Confident Thoughts' is the title. These are the Seven Thoughts of Contented Children.

These seven ideas are the foundations of self-assurance. You've won the war if you can convince your child to consider these seven things!

The Seven Confident Thoughts:

- The world is a relatively secure place.
- I can manage most situations.
- Bad things don't normally happen to me.
- It is not true that bad things appear out of nowhere.
- I have some influence over what happens to me.
- People are generally pleasant.
- Other people respect me.

Examine 'The Seven Confident Thoughts' once again.

Children who think in this way are more confident and extroverted, and they are better prepared to deal with the challenges that life throws at them. So, how do you get your kids to think like this?

This is something that many parents frequently inquire about.
Usually with a panicked expression on their faces. They exclaim, "We are not the therapist!" "We have no idea how to change someone's mind!"

But it's hardly magic to make someone think certain things. In fact, parents are unquestionably the best at it. Consider what other notions your child has. Which football team do you believe is the best in the world, according to your child? It's probably the same as Mum or Dad's.

Have you ever made your child wait for Santa Claus or the Tooth Fairy? And who implanted such notion in their minds? That's right, parents are masters at molding their children's perspectives, and they're in the ideal position to teach their children "The Seven Confident Thoughts." We may sometimes persuade children to believe something just by telling them. Sometimes we need to be a little more cunning than that. You'll have to put in some effort to persuade your child to believe in 'The Seven Confident Thoughts.'

Step One – Special Time

Every day, give your child 10 minutes of your undivided attention. Spending some additional time with your child is the first thing you can do to teach them the Seven Confident Thoughts. This is referred to as "Special Time."

You'll need to spend around ten minutes a day doing this with an anxious or sad youngster. You must obey certain simple regulations during Special Time.

Unlike a smaller child, a teenager is unlikely to want to sit down and play snap with you. A sit-down with a cup of tea and a little chat, on the other hand, will suffice. For older children, having your undivided attention and warmth for 10 minutes works wonders.

Special Time: 10 Minutes Quiz

From the Seven Confident Thoughts, which one do you believe the ten minutes of Special Time will enable your kid to improve? Mark the lines that apply to your case:

Special Time

- Make an effort to do Special Time daily.
- Find out what your child wants to do for the next 10 minutes.
- Allow them to choose whatever they want, within reason.
- Give the child your complete attention for the entire ten minutes. Turn off the TV, ignore the phone, and don't try multitasking (cooking dinner, ironing clothes simultaneously).
- Take pleasure in your time with your child. Use this moment to lavish praise on your child.

- Let the child be in charge for these 10 minutes. It's acceptable if they want to modify the rules of the game you're playing. Allow it to pass if they behave goofy or pompous. It's all about having a good time throughout these ten minutes. Don't condemn your child until they do something risky.
- There are plenty of other moments for learning, so don't use this time to teach your child. These ten minutes are solely for you and your child to enjoy each other's company.
- During these ten minutes, try not to ask too many questions.

Asking questions prevents your child's mind from relaxing and flowing. Questions are acceptable at any time, but not during this special 10-minute period.

Have a second look at the seven Confident Thoughts:

1. The world is a relatively secure place.
2. I can manage most situations.
3. Bad things don't usually happen to me.
4. Bad things don't appear out of nowhere.
5. I have some influence over what happens to me.
6. People are generally pleasant.
7. Other people respect me.

You may argue that this particular period is advantageous to all seven Confident Thoughts. However, I feel that it is most useful for these four specific points.

1. The world is a relatively secure place (your child should feel warm, protected, and calm during this Special Time)
2. I have some influence over what occurs to me (during this Special time, your child should feel in charge of what happens to them, which is an uncommon occurrence for most children)
3. People are rather polite (didn't you remember to be friendly, courteous, and pleasant?)
4. Others hold me in high regard (you have been showing your child that you respect them).

Step 2 – Have a good time with your family.
Consider this:

When was the last time you did anything enjoyable with your family? If it's been more than a week, you owe it to yourself and your family to prioritize spending quality time together. Every week, try to have at least one Happy Family Time. These occasions do not have to be costly or time-consuming. Choose something that will appeal to all of you. Here are some suggestions for having a good time with your family:

- Take a stroll in the park.
- Play card games together.
- Play a game of board together.
- Make a painting together.
- Bake a cake together.
- Plan a picnic.
- Visit a museum or art gallery – most are free today.
- Or, ask your child what they want to do and see what they come up with.

Step 3- Being able to communicate well within your family

In every family, being able to communicate well is critical. It is especially vital for a family with a child who is worried or sad.

Communicating nasty surprises

David, who was eight at the time, was terrified of the dentist.

No one knew why he was afraid of the dentist because he had never had a negative dental encounter before. On the other hand, his mother was terrified of the dentist and believed David picked up on her fear by hearing her talk about it. Anyway, whenever it was time to go to the dentist, his mother waited as long as she could before alerting David. She expected him to become enraged and create a scene. Instead, she waited until the last possible moment to inform him. Normally, she just informed him of their departure time in the morning.

This often resulted in massive outbursts and agitation, but Mum reasoned that one morning was better than a week.

- What are your thoughts?
- Was David's mother correct in not informing him until the last possible moment?

This was a question I posed to a group of parents who were attending our parents' get-together. They all agreed at the outset of the course that she was doing the correct thing by keeping the length of time he was unhappy to a minimum and that she was a caring parent. Then, at the end of the meet-up, I asked them again, and each of them provided a different response.

David's mother should have given him a couple of days' notice before they had to go to the dentist, they all agreed. When I questioned why they had changed their minds, one very wise mother, Melanie, pointed to our poster of the Seven Confident Thoughts and stated, "David has to understand that awful things don't just happen." He has to know that bad shocks aren't just around the corner if he wants to overcome his anxiety." Melanie had the support of all of the parents and mine as well.

These parents are absolutely correct. If we believe that unpleasant shocks may appear out of nowhere and bite us, we will always be on alert.

So, how much advance warning should a child receive? This is a difficult issue to answer because it is dependent on your child's age. As a general rule of thumb, I would say:

- I would attempt to offer a day or two of warning to an older child, perhaps five to seven years of age, because they don't have a clear grasp of time, and any more than a couple of hours of warning would feel like weeks away.
- If the child is between the ages of eight and eleven, I will provide several days to a week's notice.
- If your child is older than eleven, give them as much notice as possible; they have a right to know if anything bad is going to happen, and if they find out you've been concealing things from them, they may lose faith in your honesty.

Good co-parenting

Co-parenting refers to how parents collaborate to raise their children. In recent years, we've realized how critical successful co-parenting is to children's well-being. You should read this part even if you are raising your child on your own. You may be the primary caregiver for your child, but others – grandparents, childminders, and so on – normally play a role as well, and you all must work together.

Is it necessary for children to be consistent? In a nutshell, they do. When all persons who care for a child follow the same set of rules, the finest parenting occurs.

But, let's be honest, I've never known a household in which all of the adults had the same rules for the kids. It's quite natural and healthy for parents to disagree on how their children should be raised, and in most cases, one parent is a little more permissive than the other.

So, what do you do if you and the other essential persons in your child's life hold opposing viewpoints?

Discuss, discuss, discuss

The first step is to talk about the rules you desire for your children. It's a lot simpler to blend in with other people if you know what they believe. An anxious or sad child should stick to a few simple guidelines. If the other person does not agree with your rule, explain your argument politely and with a smile. Then pay attention to their reaction and think about it.

Compromise, compromise, compromise

Making little concessions is an important part of life, and if your children observe people settling their conflicts amicably by making compromises, they will learn a valuable lesson. Only a few rules are so crucial that they can't be tweaked somewhat.

I'll reveal a tiny secret to you.

Compromise is a favorite of conflict resolution psychologists. They've demonstrated via extensive study that if you make a small compromise to your opponent, they'll almost certainly reply by making a large compromise in return! So, if you want to persuade someone to agree with you, give some ground on something else. So, what if you and the other parent/grandparent/childminder disagree on something?

Sometimes we just have to accept that someone is set in their ways and that we won't be able to alter them.

Take a look at Joe's case.

Joe's parents were divorced when he was a child. They had worked really hard to keep the divorce peaceful, and they were both determined to be the best parents they could be for Joe's sake.

Human nature, however, intervened, and Joe's parents began to do things their own way. Joe's mother preferred that he take a bath every night and go to bed at 8.30 p.m., so that's what occurred while he stayed with her. Joe's father, on the other hand, was more relaxed about it. Joe was not forced to take a bath every night, and he was allowed to remain up until 9.30 or 10 p.m.

Joe's mother was furious because she was concerned that Joe would become exhausted and dirty as a result of this. You can probably predict what occurred.

Joe grumbled about having to take a bath and go to bed early while he was at Mum's place. Mum was obviously unhappy, and each time it happened, she became increasingly irritated. She eventually felt irritated and just informed Joe that she believed his father was being careless.

Do you believe Joe's mother made the correct decision? I believe we can all put ourselves in her situation and understand why she was irritated.

She was, however, doing Joe no favors by undermining his father. Children must have complete faith in their parents and think that they are capable parents. If Joe starts to believe that his father isn't good, it might aggravate his anxieties. Also, children may be trusted to go tell the other parent what was said. It's not great to hear that your ex-wife thinks you're a bad parent, and it's not going to help you establish a strong co-parenting relationship.

In conclusion, it is preferable if all of the adults in a child's life follow the same set of rules. It's fine if the rules differ somewhat. If this is the case, all of the adults must try really hard to portray to the kid that they are all working together and that, although having different rules, they respect each other's judgments.

Why not get your child's other parent to read this book as a good start to your co-parenting relationship? Everyone in the child's environment should practice the techniques presented in this book.

Also, suppose you're taking your child to visit a professional for treatment with depression or anxiety, attempt to get the aid of other significant family members. In that case, often, the therapist will offer counsel to the family, and it is much more effective if everyone follows it.

CHAPTER 10: BOOSTING YOUR CHILD'S SELF-ESTEEM AND CONFIDENCE

Remember how I introduced the notion of the Seven Confident Thoughts in previous chapters? We've previously discussed how you can use time with your child to encourage these views, and we'll look at how you can handle your child's problematic behavior in the best manner possible to guarantee that they grow up thinking this way.

In this chapter, we'll look at some more things you can do to help your child's confidence and self-esteem through the Seven Confident Thoughts.

The Seven Confident Thoughts:

- The world is a relatively secure place.
- I can manage most situations.
- Bad things don't usually happen to me.
- It is not true that bad things appear out of nowhere.
- I have some influence over what happens to me.
- People are generally pleasant.
- Other people respect me.

Make the most of your child's abilities.

Everyone appears to lead at some things. These things seem to come a little more effortlessly to certain people than to others. What are your child's most significant assets? When I mention strengths, I'm not referring to skills that your child excels at. It is not necessary to win an Olympic medal or to graduate with a Ph.D. for anything to be one of your strengths. It just has to be something you enjoy doing and have an aptitude for.

We all need something that we are good at if we want to have high self-esteem. If you can't think of many things, this is likely to contribute to your child's problems majorly.

So, what do you do when you're stuck on ideas? The first step is to see whether there is anything you could have overlooked. Ask your friends, family, and teachers if there is anything you've overlooked: some small distinctive features that you may have overlooked may have been observed by others.

When you've figured out what your child excels in, the next step is to use them to enhance their self-esteem. It's not as complicated as it appears. However, if your child suffers from anxiety or depression, you will need to put in a little additional effort.

So, what do I have to do?

It's simple. Take a nice long look at the list of beautiful traits you've made for your child, and then praise, praise, praise every time you find your child doing one of the items on the list! Your goal is to express your pride in your child and let them know that they possess highly valued attributes.

For the next twenty-four hours, I want to issue you a challenge.

I'd like you to attempt to compliment your child on at least five of the traits on the list. Of course, you may compliment them on other areas as well, even things they aren't really strong at but have made an effort to improve. However, children must learn about the strengths in which they are exceptional.

Push them to try new things

One of the first things that come to mind when we are nervous or sad is to go back into our shells. We stop attempting new things, we get complacent, and we cease doing many of the things we used to do. This is a severe issue. Anxious or depressed children already have a negative opinion of themselves. They believe they are incapable of dealing with situations and that no one can help them.

Allow them to experience how it feels to try new things (it usually feels great) and prove that they are capable of amazing things when they put their minds to it.

So, get your kids involved in some new fun activities. Of course, getting a reluctant child to take up a recent action is easier said than done.

CHAPTER 11: BEHAVIORAL MODIFICATIONS TO MANAGE AN ANXIOUS CHILD

Learning to control poor and nervous behavior

Many parents with anxious or depressive children are irritated by compliments such as "What a nice little boy!" or "What a well-behaved young lady she is!" from others. While their children are usually well-behaved outside of the comfort of their own houses, they may be absolute nightmares within their own families. This chapter offers advice on coping with anxious children's challenging behaviors.

When therapists see parents in their clinics, they always teach the ways of increasing good behaviors before they go on to dealing with the less desirable behaviors. I have done this in the careful ordering of this book too. Some parents find this frustrating. A frequent plea in the early stages of our parent groups is, "When are you going to tell us how to deal with the really annoying behaviors? – that's what we really want to hear." Parents begin to come in with beautiful stories after a few weeks of using the approaches for developing better and daring behavior.

"I can't believe it; I haven't even started dealing with Jordan's fighting, and it's almost entirely gone away — he's a transformed child!". When you think about it, the explanation for this is apparent. When children can obtain lovely, positive interactions from their parents just by being good, they are less likely to want to attract your attention by being bad.

Many families, however, discover that despite completing all of the excellent parenting activities — spending time with their children, playing with them, praising and rewarding them, and so on, their children continue to exhibit behaviors that their parents wish to modify.

In the past, most parents who come for counseling have dealt with these behaviors by yelling, hitting, or employing some other kind of severe punishment. By the time they've been in parent support groups for a few weeks, they've realized that these approaches don't work and are really harmful to anxious or depressed children. So, what methods may parents employ instead? Ignoring, Time Out, and Consequences are the three abilities discussed in this chapter for parents. However, do not use these strategies until you are satisfied that your child can acquire all the attention they require by being friendly and confident.

Ignoring

As you may have guessed, the one thing that all children crave (and want) is adult attention, particularly from their parents. For nervous and depressed children, this requirement is considerably larger. This can be a big annoyance, but you can use it to your advantage if you're a wise parent.

We discussed how praise might be used to encourage positive and self-assured behaviors. Why is praising so beneficial in this situation? Praise is a sort of highly excellent, powerful parental attention, and if a behavior gets your child noticed, you can bet they'll do it again and again.

It also operates the opposite way around, which is beneficial to us. If a behavior goes unnoticed, you can be sure that your child will become bored with it very quickly. As a result, we educate the parents who come to us on the method of ignoring. Some of them are skeptical at first, but once they get the feel of it, they can't stop themselves. In the case study below, a humorous small case example is provided.

Henry was seven years old, and, in addition to being a nervous child, he had a strong temper. He had mastered some relatively crude terms at school and relished the opportunity to show off his linguistic prowess in a polite society.

He would swear profanely if his mother irritated him (by not allowing him to do what he wanted). His mother would scold him, visibly ashamed. Henrey's mother chose to try ignoring after I introduced the attention rule to her. When Henry swore, she was to turn away from him, say nothing, not look at him, and completely ignore him until he calmed down. She knew it would be terribly difficult since she was embarrassed by Henry's behavior, but she decided to try to ignore it because the swearing was not causing any harm. When she returned the following week, she informed me that the first two days had been terrible — she had done a fantastic job of ignoring Henry's yelling – but it was almost as if he had tried harder to grab her attention. But she persisted, and by day three, he was swearing less and less. By day four, it had almost totally disappeared, and Henry had not sworn in three days.

The rules for Ignoring

When should I use ignorance?

Ignoring may be used to deal with practically any undesirable behavior. It's particularly effective for grumbling, whining, nagging, tantrums, and cursing.

When should I not use ignorance?

The only time you should not ignore it is if the behavior is harmful and someone may be injured.

Also, don't ignore your child's behavior if it's potentially detrimental (unless it's their own stuff, of course). They are free to make their own decisions in this regard.

So, where do I go from here?

Once you've decided to ignore a behavior (such as swearing), make a concerted effort to ignore it every time it occurs; it will clear up far more rapidly than if you merely ignore it sometimes.

When you're not paying attention:

• Avoid looking at your child.

• Do not communicate with your child.

• Keep your distance from your child.

• It's typically better to look away from your child and concentrate on something else, such as cleaning or reading a magazine. If necessary, walk into a separate room while leaving the child alone.

• As soon as your child begins to behave nicely, praise them for it and stop ignoring them.
• If the unpleasant behavior returns, repeat the process of ignoring it.

Things to be on the lookout for:

• Beware! Things may grow worse before they get better.

• When you start neglecting your child, they won't realize you're serious and will try even harder to win your attention. DO NOT GIVE UP... IT WILL BE WORTH IT.

• Check to see whether you're genuinely ignoring.

• One of the most typical blunders made by parents is starting a conversation with their child midway through. "I'm ignoring you... I'm not listening," parents have said to their children. Of course, as soon as you do so, the child is aware that they have your undivided attention, and you are doomed.

• As soon as your child begins to behave nicely, praise them for it and stop ignoring them.

• If the unpleasant behavior returns, repeat the process of ignoring it.

• Develop the ability to make quick judgments.

If you have a headstrong child, tolerating negative behavior for the first few times might be exhausting. Unfortunately, suppose parents give in after ignoring their children for a time. In that case, they are just teaching their children that if they persevere in their poor behavior, they will ultimately get the attention they need - something no parent wants to teach their children!

This means that if you give in, the next time you have to do the work will be more difficult.

As a result, we always advise parents to make a quick judgment on whether or not they can carry out the Ignoring. If you determine you aren't up to the task of ignoring something to the finish, give in.

• It can be hard for the first time.

• Ignoring is difficult at first, but with practice, it becomes easier. It will most likely be quite tricky the first time you try it. So, when you first do this, make sure you have everything on your side. For example, it's probably better if you don't try ignoring for the first time on a Saturday morning. When you have lots of time and are feeling calm and in control, try it at home.

Managing potentially harmful and damaging behaviors:

Time Out

So, ignoring unpleasant but innocuous behaviors works well, but what about those hazardous, aggressive behaviors that might cause someone or something harm? Time Out is a practical approach to cope with this. You've probably heard of Time Out. You might have even tried it.

You could even sigh as you read this. But keep reading. Time Out is a challenging technique, and it's easy to get wrong if you haven't been taught it properly. It may, however, become a very gentle and effective technique of punishing an anxious or depressed child if a few fundamental principles are followed.

Time Out is excellent for children between the ages of 18 months and ten years.

Time Out is a form of super-ignorance. If your child does something harmful or damaging, they will be placed in a calm and uninteresting environment. For a few minutes, they can relax and reflect on their activities.

How do you take time out?

1. Select a location for your child to sit during Time Out. Make sure it's a highly dull environment — don't use their bedroom because it's full of intriguing stuff, and bedrooms are supposed to be connected with good times. Some parents use the stairwell or go to the restroom. Make sure, however, that you select a secure location.
2. Don't allow your child to use time out to avoid doing anything they're afraid of.
3. If your child refuses to stop, put them in Time Out immediately. Explain that you're bringing them to Time Out because what they did was illegal, hazardous, or otherwise

inappropriate. Take them by the arm firmly or politely if necessary and force them to go to Time Out.

4. In Time Out, keep your focus to a bare minimum. If you don't have to, don't look at them, talk to them, or touch them.

5. Place your child in Time Out for 5 minutes if they are five or older. Keep them in Time Out for one minute for each year of their lives if they are under the age of five. They remain for three minutes if they are three, four minutes if they are four, and so on. Children may exit time Out before the time limit has expired.

Dealing with non-compliance: What Happens If You Don't Follow the Rules?

Time Out is effective for more aggressive behaviors, but it should be used only when necessary. It loses its potency if you use it too much. It also doesn't work well with teens and older children. Ignoring helps deal with annoying behaviors, but what about when your child refuses to do what you want them to? Is it possible to ignore this? The answer is, of course, no. What are the chances that they will actually go and tidy their room if you urge them to do something, "Please go and tidy your room immediately," and then ignore them?

So, if your child is disobedient, or if you find yourself utilizing time Out too frequently, consider employing a strategy we term "consequences."

Remember to try all of the positive tactics first - does your child know that if they follow directions, they will be praised? Can you give your child a modest incentive if they follow your instructions?

Consequences

When your child is taught that if they don't do as instructed, they will lose a privilege, this is known as consequences. Consequences are appropriate for children and teens of all ages. However, some very young children (under four) may find it challenging to comprehend.

Consequences and how to manage them

1. Give your child a warning before imposing the penalty; for example, "Go put your bike in the garage immediately, or you won't be able to ride your bike for the rest of the day."
2. Issue only one warning. If they do not follow instructions, they will suffer the consequences. "Because you haven't put your bike away, you won't be able to ride it for the remainder of the day."
3. Try to make the decision as quickly as possible - the same day or the next day. The younger the child is, the more vital this is. If you delay the consequence (for example, "You can't go swimming next weekend"), the child may have forgotten what the penalty is for by the time you arrive, and you may find yourself letting them off the hook.

4. Never impose a severe, cruel, or terrifying punishment. It should irritate the child, but not to the point of distressing or frightening them.
5. Never issue a penalty that takes away a child's fundamental rights, such as "You can't go to school today because you didn't clean up" or "You're going to bed without food because you didn't clean up."
6. Make sure the consequence is one you can live with.
7. Once you've made a decision, stick with it! If you let your child off the hook for punishment, they will believe that they can get away with breaking the rules.

Consequences, both positive and negative

Beneficial consequences

- "The television is switched off for half an hour."

- "For the remainder of the day, there will be no PlayStation."

- "You won't be able to see the match on television this afternoon."

- "At this point, we'll have to leave the park and return home."

- "You'll have to undertake some extra household duties" (but make sure that this is something that you know you can make them do).

- "On the walk home from school today, there will be no sweets."

Negative Consequences

- "We're going to cut our vacation short and return home right now."

- "You're going to bed right now."

- "When your father gets home, I'll inform him."

- "I'll give away your beloved cat."

- "You're not going on the field trip next week."

- "You'll be grounded for two weeks."

- "You're not going to get any dinner."

Answers to the quiz on Bad Consequences

We're going to cut our vacation short and return home right now.
This is problematic because it is a hollow threat that is nearly hard to carry out. As a result, the child will not believe the parents' warnings, which is not a scenario you want to find yourself in.

If you decide to stick to your decision and carry it out (as one family I know did), you will face a massive penalty out of proportion to the crime, not just for the child but for the entire family.

It caused a lot of bitterness and hostility in this family, and it took a long time for everyone to trust each other again.

You're going to bed right now.
There are two issues with this one. First and foremost, the bed should be a peaceful and enjoyable environment. If a bed is used as a punishment, the child may begin to dislike going to bed and may develop sleeping issues as a result. Second, it can be out of proportion with the offense, primarily if employed before nightfall, resulting in a lengthy Time Out.

When your father returns home, I'll inform him.
There are several issues here. To begin with, it implies that the consequence does not occur immediately, and in reality, the child has no idea what the result will be, so they worry about it for the rest of the day. Second, it portrays Dad as the "big bad wolf," which is detrimental to his relationship with his child. Third, it teaches the child that their mother is incapable of dealing with their behavior. Fourth, by the Time Dad arrives, Mum has generally forgotten about it, so nothing occurs. Finally, Dad was not there at the time of the offense, making him not the right person to deal with it.

I'll give away your beloved cat.

It is harsh to use this as punishment unless provided because the child is not properly caring for the cat. It will cause the child much distress and resentment against the parent. These notions are especially harmful to anxious children.

Next week's school excursion will be canceled due to your absence.

There are two points to be made here. It is too far away to be truly effective. By the time it comes around, a younger child will have forgotten what the punishment is for (so it won't help them change their behavior), and an older child will be resentful of you for a week, which isn't ideal when you're trying to establish a tranquil family.

For the next two weeks, you will be grounded.

There are several issues here. To begin with, it is really severe. Second, will this parent be able to keep up with everything? What does the child learn if the parent relents after a few days? Finally, the family will be tense and resentful, which will be challenging for sensitive children.

There will be no dinner for you.

Even if a child has been particularly misbehaving, it is never appropriate for a parent to deprive them of their fundamental rights. Denying a child food, education, medical care, or sleep should never be utilized unless you want a Social Services visit!

CHAPTER 12: DEALING WITH WORRY AND FEARS

Childhood is filled with fears and anxieties. Consider all of the children you are familiar with. Is there anyone you can think of who hasn't experienced separation anxiety? (When a child is separated from their primary caregiver, they experience separation anxiety.) This period, which begins around the age of eight months, is totally natural for young children. It would be much odd if a child did not experience it. Similarly, pre-school children frequently develop phobias of monsters, ghosts, the dark, and other such things.

There is a cause for these anxieties and fears. Fears like these, according to psychologists, have an evolutionary function. If a child screams when he is removed from his mother, it signifies that she has a strong chance of hearing the screams and will be able to find him again if she genuinely has lost him.

Similarly, teens are approaching the time where they are becoming more self-reliant from their parents. As a result, now is the time for them to improve their ability to work with others. If they are concerned about their popularity, this will motivate them to improve their social skills. Teenagers are also nearing the end of their reproductive time.

Those concerned about their beauty in the past would have taken the most care of their appearance, attracting the most acceptable partners and having the most offspring. Of course, we don't want our kids to start breeding at 15, but that is what our bodies were designed to accomplish.

Fears

So, while worries are frequent throughout childhood, most children appear to grow out of them. Why don't some kids grow out of them? I believe the answer is complicated, but a large part of it rests in two fundamental processes known as 'avoidance' and the 'fight-flight response, as defined by psychologists.

Avoidance

We know that when sensitive children are confronted with something terrifying, they typically flee. Usually, well-intentioned parents assist them in this. For example, a caring parent would frequently tell me that they let their child sleep in their bed with them since the child is afraid of sleeping alone. However, this benevolence may result in particular issues. The problem is that by avoiding the item they are scared of; children miss out on the opportunity to see if it is genuinely terrifying.

A child who never sleeps in their bed, for example, will never learn that the monsters under the bed aren't going to come out and eat them in the middle of the night!

Second, by assisting the child in avoiding the thing they are afraid of, the parent may be sending a subliminal message that "yes, sleeping on your own is harmful." This is regarded as avoidance by psychologists, and it is crucial to comprehending anxiety. The case study below demonstrates how departure can lead to the development of phobias.

Kelly's parents took her to visit a psychotherapist when she was 12 years old because she was afraid of snakes. This is a pretty common phobia, and it seldom creates significant issues for people living in urban areas. On the other hand, Kelly lived in a rural region with a lot of grass snakes, and her anxiety had grown to the point that she couldn't go outdoors. Kelly's phobia had started when she was much younger. She'd seen something on TV about people being bitten by snakes, and it had made her quite concerned. She was out for a stroll with her parents a few days later when she came upon a grass snake. She grew so distressed that her father had to take her up and carry her home. Kelly made a big deal about not going near where she had seen the snake from then on. Whenever they went anywhere near there, her father had to carry her. The commotion eventually became too much for the family, and they avoided going near that region at all costs.

Kelly's dread became more significant over time, and she refused to go on family walks at all, especially during the time of year when snakes were most active.

When Kelly's relatives managed to pull her out for walks, they were typically cut short when she became irritated.

Can you see how Kelly's phobia developed from her fear? Kelly's kind-hearted family understood the snakes couldn't hurt her, but they didn't want to see her sad (and to be honest, neither did her mother), so they let her keep out of the path of snakes. Kelly had several anxieties about what would happen if she came across a snake, including that it would bite her, that it would creep into her hair and clothes, and that she would be so terrified that she would get ill. Of course, none of this was correct, but Kelly had no way of knowing.

As you can see from Kelly's therapy, it's pretty unusual for a psychologist to advise a child to abandon their avoidance and face their darkest fears head-on. Fears were once handled in this way: a person afraid of spiders would be placed in a room with many spiders. However, we now know that this generally causes more harm than benefit, and people are advised to reduce their avoidance wherever feasible gradually.

Treating Miranda

Deirdre, the psychologist, and Kelly began constructing a "fear hierarchy" after spending some time getting to know one other. A fear hierarchy is a list of the things you're afraid of (in this example, snakes), with the least frightening item at the bottom and the most terrifying item at the top.

Miranda's hierarchy looked like this:

• Step 9: Taking care and observing a live snake.

• Step 8: Getting up and touching a live snake.

• Step 7: Observe a live snake.

• Step 6: Entering a room containing a live snake.

• Step 5: Watching a snake on television.

• Step 4: Examining snake images.

• Step 3: Studying realistic snake drawings.

• Step 2: Studying snake cartoon drawings.

• Step 1: Look at some pretty lousy snake stick drawings.

To begin, Derek sketched some dreadful, scribbly snake drawings hoping that Kelly would be bold enough to look at them. Kelly was uneasy, but she managed to sit down and look at the images. Derek persuaded her to sit for 15 minutes and stare at them. Kelly stated that she felt good after the 15 minutes and was no longer bothered by the photographs. This method of overcoming anxiety by spending time with the fear is called 'habituation,' and it is pretty successful.

Derek then persuaded Kelly to look at some cartoon snake illustrations they had discovered in a children's book. Kelly stated that she felt alright within 15 minutes. With Kelly's family's aid, Kelly and Derek made their way up the fear hierarchy over the next few weeks. Kelly's father arranged for Kelly to go to his colleague's house for the final few steps. His co-worker had a snake as a pet and had agreed to let her view it. Despite her anxiety, she was fearless and worked her way to the top of her fear hierarchy, even managing to hold the snake for a few minutes. Kelly had overcome her phobia and was now ready to walk outside without the worry of seeing a grass snake! Her family ensured that her aversion would not resurface by providing several opportunities to meet grass snakes and learn that they would not harm her.

The Fight-Flight Response

It is another psychological mechanism that I believe is important in the development of fears and phobias. I want you to think back to a time when people lived in caves.

"You're a tiny caveman out hunting for lunch. But you're not the only one seeking food, and as you turn a corner, you come face to face with a big, ravenous saber-toothed tiger! So, what exactly do you do? In such a situation, most individuals would do the same thing: flee as quickly as possible. Our bodies must prepare themselves for action to escape from the tiger. As a result, we begin to release adrenaline, which causes our hearts to pump blood to our muscles and our lungs to expand.

Meanwhile, all of the blood pushed into our muscles to dash needs to come from someplace. As a result, the young caveman's body diverts blood away from his stomach and skin. These organs can go without blood for a while. Unfortunately, all of this physical activity has some negative consequences — it may be exhausting. The caveman's knees are wobbly, his breathing is short and rapid, he is nauseous, and his stomach is churning, his mind is foggy, and he may be sweating, and he seems pale and unwell.

Is there anything that all of this reminds you of? Great! If you notice that your child looks just like this when they are scared, this is because, even though we live in the twenty-first century, our bodies are still formed for the stone era. We no longer have to contend with saber-toothed tigers; instead, we must deal with school, groups of people, homework, dark restrooms, and so on. Unfortunately, our bodies and minds have not caught up, and we still react to our concerns in the same manner that the tiny caveman did - by preparing to flee.

Unfortunately, there isn't much we can do about it. This is the way our bodies are built, and we have no choice but to accept it. However, children and their parents must realize that none of these sentiments may harm them in any way. These sensations are our bodies preparing for a long run, and you don't see many obese marathon runners, do you? When your child is terrified, they may appear and feel bad, but they are not harming themselves in any way. They need to be reassured that they are protected.

Tips for Dealing with fears

It's essential to overcome a fear or phobia with caution and patience, but it's relatively straightforward.

1. As Kelly and Derek did, create a "fear hierarchy" with your child. A blank worksheet is available.
2. Ensure that the transitions from one level to the next are small. If you make a step that is too huge, your child may not complete it. If you're unsure, start with tiny steps. It doesn't matter if there are four stages of forty-four, as long as each one is manageable for your child.
3. Start with the first level.
4. Please encourage your child to face their fears for 15 minutes. Miranda spent 15 minutes working on the snake drawings. Reassure your child that, no matter how bad they are feeling, they are only human.
5. When your child has completed this level, lavish them with praise. Consider rewarding them with a modest prize.
6. Proceed to the next level if your child is ready. Carry on in the same manner as previously mentioned.
7. If your child appears tired or irritable, skip it for another different time.

There is one uncommon exception: certain persons who have a blood phobia will pass out if they sight blood. In this instance, the blood pressure drops unexpectedly, and the person may pass out.

If this has never occurred to your child before, it is unlikely to happen now, and you should feel confident in assuring them that they are well and will not faint.

Draw a fear hierarchy for one of your child's fears.

- Step 10

_____

- Step 9

_____

- Step 8

_____

- Step 7

_____

- Step 6

_____

- Step 5

_____

- Step 4

_____

- Step 3

_____

- Step 2

_____

- Step 1

_____

TIPS:

• Begin by completing Step 1. Make it as simple as possible.

• Then proceed to Step 10. Make this your ultimate objective.

• Fill in the gaps between the stages. Make each step a little bit more complex than the one before it.

• There doesn't have to be ten stages; it may be three, twenty, or anywhere in between.

• When your child does this, they will be completely reliant on you for assistance. So, whatever you do, keep a cheerful attitude. Do not criticize them in any way, even if they are grumpy or sluggish. If you are not in a patient mindset, you'll need to be patient first, and this is not the moment to complete the fear hierarchy. Get someone else to do it or put it off till later.

•Your child will be searching for safety indicators' from you. Anxious children do this all the time, and they don't even realize it. They're always looking at you to check if you believe the setting is secure. They will perceive your horrified or crying expression as "oh no, Mum is worried — it must be harmful." This is not a good situation! So, if you're not feeling well, you'll have to fake it here! With a big confident smile and a calm voice, you're ready to go!

Worries

We're all concerned. It's pretty natural. It is critical to remember this and understand that worry cannot harm you, no matter how unpleasant it may seem. Worrying has a poor reputation thanks to phrases like "I was going insane with worry" and "he worried himself to death." Worrying will not drive you insane or kill you. On the other hand, excessive worrying may be unpleasant, and if you have a child who appears to be concerned about everything all of the time, this section will give you some advice on how to cope with it.

I'm going to divide worry into two categories: Each has a somewhat different approach to the problem.

They're referred to as reasonable and unrealistic anxieties, respectively. Real worries are the kinds of anxieties that arise daily as a result of real-life issues. For example, a child who is struggling in school may be concerned that he may fail a test. A child who has been subjected to teasing or bullying may be worried about being tormented at school tomorrow.

In general, I refer to fear as realistic if it has a decent likelihood of coming true. Not all problems, however, fall into this category. If your kid is worried or depressed, many of their fears are likely to be unreasonable. These are fears that are extremely unlikely to be realized. "If I fail my test, my instructor will spank me," or "all of the students at school despise me," or "going to the dentist will be excruciatingly painful."

Dealing with realistic worries

The best method to deal with real worries is to sit down with your child and figure out what you can do to help them solve their situation. For instance, if they are afraid about failing a test, you may devise a revision strategy (perhaps with some bit of rewards built-in). If they are so scared of being teased, you may assist in resolving the issue by speaking with the school and devising techniques for coping with the taunting. Sometimes these concerns are just difficulties that an anxious or depressed child perceives to be overly large. Lucy, in the case study, has a similar situation. In this instance, you and your child should sit down with a piece of paper and divide the problem into manageable chunks.

Dealing with unrealistic worries

We sometimes worry about things that aren't likely to happen. For example, many children are concerned that their instructor will yell at them if they perform poorly on a test or complete their homework to a poor standard.

While it's true that their instructor may be disappointed and want to talk to your child to figure out what's wrong, teachers nowadays shouldn't be yelling at students.

Lucy, who was twelve years old at the time, she was highly concerned about a significant scientific test she was scheduled to take at school. Lucy's mother felt she'd be alright as long as she did a tiny amount of revision. However, despite her anxiety, Lucy didn't appear to know how to address the situation. Lucy and her mother thus got down and made a list of what Lucy needed to do to fix her problem.

It appeared as follows:

1. Check your assignment book to see what the test will be about.

2. Make a list of all the subjects Lucy needs to revise.

3. Divide the topics to look at one or two each night before the test.

4. Set aside half an hour each night to read over the topic for that night(s).

5. Have Mum give Lucy a five-minute quiz on the themes she has read about each night.

6. As a bonus, Lucy watches MTV for half an hour every night after the quiz.

Lucy's mother wanted her daughter to learn how to solve her difficulties, so she didn't merely make this list for her. Instead, she assisted Lucy in completing the task, but she pushed her to come up with her answer to the extent feasibly. It was Mum's brilliant idea to include a small prize each night as a reward for Lucy's hard work.

CONCLUSION

I hope you found this book helpful in dealing with your child's anxiety issues. However, suppose you are still having problems after reading it and attempting to practice some of the advice I have given you. In that case, I strongly advise you to seek professional assistance for your child.

Even if your child appears to be doing well, it's vital to remember that everyone experiences anxiety and despair at times. We all go through periods of depression or times when we have a lot of worries. This is natural, and you should not be alarmed if your child experiences it from time to time.

At the same time, it's crucial to remember that a child who has been nervous or sad before is more likely to have the same problems again. It's a good idea to stay continuing with all of the techniques you've learned to employ to reduce the chances of recurrence. Don't forget to shower your child with praise when they exhibit positive, self-assured behavior. When kids exhibit behaviors that their parents cannot accept, remember to employ positive disciplinary techniques such as light penalties and time out. Above all, please don't give up on spending everyday pleasant, quality time with them. This is something that all children require, but your child needs it more than others.

If your child begins to revert to previous habits, have a positive attitude. Allowing oneself to get pulled down with them is not a good idea. They want you to believe that they can overcome the obstacles once more. Please return to the techniques you learned in this book and make sure you're using them regularly.

Resources

[1] Sahiner, N. C., & Bal, M. D. (2016). The effects of three different distraction methods on pain and anxiety in children. *Journal of Child Health Care, 20*(3), 277-285.

[1] Green, S. A., Berkovits, L. D., & Baker, B. L. (2015). Symptoms and development of anxiety in children with or without intellectual disability. *Journal of Clinical Child & Adolescent Psychology, 44*(1), 137-144.

[1] Adams D, Emerson LM. The impact of anxiety in children on the autism spectrum. Journal of Autism and Developmental Disorders. 2021 Jun;51(6):1909-20.

[1] Green, S. A., Berkovits, L. D., & Baker, B. L. (2015). Symptoms and development of anxiety in children with or without intellectual disability. *Journal of Clinical Child & Adolescent Psychology, 44*(1), 137-144.

[1] Kranzler, A., Young, J. F., Hankin, B. L., Abela, J. R., Elias, M. J., & Selby, E. A. (2016). Emotional awareness: A transdiagnostic predictor of depression and anxiety for children and adolescents. *Journal of Clinical Child & Adolescent Psychology, 45*(3), 262-269.

[1] Kerns, C. M., Winder-Patel, B., Iosif, A. M., Nordahl, C. W., Heath, B., Solomon, M., & Amaral, D. G. (2020). Clinically significant anxiety in children with autism spectrum disorder and varied intellectual functioning. *Journal of Clinical Child & Adolescent Psychology*, 1-16.

[1] Green, S. A., Berkovits, L. D., & Baker, B. L. (2015). Symptoms and development of anxiety in children with or without intellectual disability. *Journal of Clinical Child & Adolescent Psychology, 44*(1), 137-144.

[11] Ekinci, O., Titus, J. B., Rodopman, A. A., Berkem, M., & Trevathan, E. (2009). Depression and anxiety in children and adolescents with epilepsy: prevalence, risk factors, and treatment. *Epilepsy & Behavior*, *14*(1), 8-18.

[11] Yaffe, Y. (2018). Establishing specific links between parenting styles and the s-anxieties in children: Separation, social, and school. *Journal of Family Issues*, *39*(5), 1419-1437.

[1] Bögels, S. M., van Dongen, L., & Muris, P. (2003). Family influences on dysfunctional thinking in anxious children. *Infant and Child Development: An International Journal of Research and Practice*, *12*(3), 243-252.

[1] Zhang, H., Zhang, Y., Yang, L., Yuan, S., Zhou, X., Pu, J., ... & Xie, P. (2017). Efficacy and acceptability of psychotherapy for anxious young children: a meta-analysis of randomized controlled trials. *The Journal of nervous and mental disease*, *205*(12), 931-941.

[1] Spielmans, G. I., Pasek, L. F., & McFall, J. P. (2007). What are the active ingredients in cognitive and behavioral psychotherapy for anxious and depressed children? A meta-analytic review. *Clinical Psychology Review*, *27*(5), 642-654.

[1] McCurry, C. (2009). *Parenting your anxious child with mindfulness and acceptance: A powerful new approach to overcoming fear, panic, and worry using acceptance and commitment therapy*. New Harbinger Publications.

[1] Silverman, W. K., La Greca, A. M., & Wasserstein, S. (1995). What do children worry about? Worries and their relation to anxiety. *Child development*, *66*(3), 671-686.

www.ingramcontent.com/pod-product-compliance
Lightning Source LLC
LaVergne TN
LVHW012109070526
838202LV00056B/5684